OF LIVERPOOL

Two)

y

Whale

EDITION

T ST.HELENS LIBRARIES T, MERSEYSIDE.

Acknowledgements

The author thanks the copyright holders of the photographs and illustrations used in this book — particularly the Daily Post and Echo — and also those whom it has not been possible to trace.

First Printed 1984
Second Edition 1985

ISBN 0 901314 25 0

PRINTED BY T. STEPHENSON & SONS LTD., PRESCOT, MERSEYSIDE.

AINTREE & FAZAKERLEY

AINTREE, Ayntree or Ayntre, as this district was sometimes written in ancient documents, means "One Tree," and is taken from the Anglo-Saxon "an-treow." Why there should be such a relatively large area, so close to the heavily-forested West Derby, about 1,000 years ago, with only one tree, seems to be a mystery today. However, in the far future, Aintree's flat and open landscape proved to be a bonus for it not only became an important place for horse-racing but also for flying, and a number of pioneer flights were made from here.

The whole world, of course, knows that Aintree is the home of the Grand National. Not so many, however, would know that there was horse racing on the flat in this area when Elizabeth I was on the throne. Steeple-chasing was introduced at nearby Maghull in 1837 (when Victoria came to the throne) and, two years later, on February 26, the Grand National, then known as the Liverpool Grand Steeple Chase, was run at Aintree.

It was chiefly through the efforts of William Lynn, sporting proprietor of the Waterloo Hotel, Liverpool, that the 'chase venue was transferred in 1839 to Aintree. He was supported by a syndicate of the Earls of Derby, Sefton, Eglington and Wilton, Lord George Betlinck, Lord Stanley, Lord Robert Grosvenor and seven other well-known northern sportsmen. The race was handicapped in 1843 and renamed Grand National Steeple Chase.

The first stone of the grandstand at the new Aintree Racecourse was laid by Lord Molyneux on February 7, 1829, and the first races there took place on July 7, the same year.

All roads seemed to lead to Aintree that week and the highways were crowded with traffic, from stylish carriages-and-four to humble shandrydans — and, of course, thousands of equestrians and pedestrians.

According to the Liverpool Weekly Mercury: "The canal also furnished its quota of visitors from Liverpool, Ormskirk, Wigan and etc., and flats, packets and fly-boats, decorated with streamers and enlivened by bands of musicians came freighted with the lovers of sport. On Tuesday (opening day) there could not have been fewer than thirty to forty thousand persons on the ground".

The first race to be run on the new course was the 1¼-mile Croxteth Stakes, won by Mufti, owned by Mr. Francis.

For 70 years there was a red-brick county police station at the entrance to Aintree Racecourse. This was closed in October, 1965, and demolished to make way for an extension of the dual carriageway of the main Liverpool-Preston road.

Long before Speke and Hooton became aerodromes for flying displays, old-time fliers would unpack their crated, flimsy aircraft at Aintree Racecourse, put them together and thrill Merseysiders with their daring flights — sometimes to be measured in only yards! In November 1909, when flying was still very much in its infancy, the Daily Post and Mercury encouraged those "daring young men in their flying machines" and supported flying demonstrations there.

Sir William Pickles Hartley, the famous jam manufacturer with the large factory at Aintree, offered a £1,000 prize for the first flight from Liverpool to Manchester. Ace aviator Colonel Samuel Cody (not related to Buffalo Bill), who

brought his bi-plane in sections from Doncaster, nearly won this prize. He got as far as Eccleston Park, only ten miles from the city, but with fog preventing his seeing obstructions (like telegraph poles and wires), he was compelled to return. There were no such things as instrument-landings, talk-downs and sophisticated aids to navigation in those days, when one virtually "flew by the seat of his pants".

The famous Liverpool pioneer airman, Henry G. Melly, made it in 1911. He flew to Manchester in 49 minutes and back in 65 minutes on July 7. Henry was accompanied by his wife, Ellen, who is thought to have been the first woman to fly in Britain (other than balloonists).

Other pilots who gave public exhibitions of flying in their weird and wonderful planes at that time included the Rev. Sidney Swann, Rector of Crosby, Ravensworth, a former Cambridge rowing blue, in a monoplane designed by himself and constructed by the Austin Motor Company. Brazilian Alberto Santos Dumont, the first man to fly an aeroplane in Europe, in 1906, flew his 6½ cwt. "La Demoiselle". Mr. James More, the Scottish pilot and racing driver, had a Voisin bi-plane, like those also owned by Messrs. Simpson and Cockburn.

A sketch of the inauguration of the most famous horse race in the world – the Grand National, although in 1839, when the race was held at Aintree, it was called the Liverpool Grand Steeple Chase. The runners are seen here tackling the cruel real stone wall. During this race, Captain Becher, on Conrad, tumbled into a brook obstacle, which from then on was always known as Becher's Brook. The race was won by Lottery, whose jockey was named Mason.

But Cody seemed to be the favourite. He flew a bi-plane with a three-wheeled undercarriage and a wheel under each wing. On his first flight he managed to cover only three miles before making a forced-landing in a ploughed field at Melling, 500 yards from the railway station. Cody immediately telephoned his helpers at Aintree and said: "All's well. Landed at Melling. Send two sparking plugs." Two of the aircraft's five wheels were buckled when he again crash-landed on his return to Aintree.

During the following Great War, aircraft were considerably improved and numerous Bristol planes were turned out at Aintree's National Aircraft Factory, which had its own landing field, nudging the racecourse. From this field, on April 30, 1924, the Belfast-Liverpool airmail service was inaugurated.

It was operated by De Havilland 50's of that company's aeroplane-hire service, and crack flier Mr. (later Sir) Alan Cobham piloted the first aircraft from Belfast (Malone) to Liverpool (Aintree). He brought with him the Lord Mayor of Belfast (Ald. Sir W. Turner) and the High Sheriff (Councillor M. C. McLaurin), and waiting at Aintree to greet them at 2.40 p.m. were Sir Archibald Salvidge, deputising for the Lord Mayor; Mr. F. C. Wilson and the Town Clerk, Mr. Walter Moon. The weather was bad, with rain and mist, and the flight took 2 hours 20 minutes. But Cobham made the return flight at 5.30 p.m., via Southport sand (to pick up newspapers) in only two hours. The aircraft carried four passengers (fares were £3 single). They cruised at 95 m.p.h. and had a range of 380 miles. An aircraft left Liverpool at 5.15 a.m. and Belfast at 6.20 p.m., on this daily service. Letters from Belfast were delivered in Liverpool the same evening and in London and provincial towns, the next morning. Poor

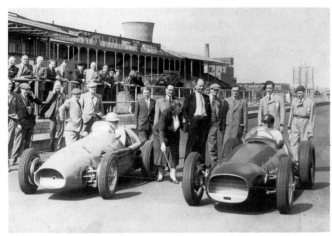

Mrs. Mirabel Topham, late owner of Aintree Racecourse, flags out Ken Wharton in a B.R.M. for the first test run on the new Aintree motor track, in May, 1954. Reg. Parnell watches from his Ferrari.

weather conditions at that time, and sparse aerodrome facilities, caused this service to be cancelled. It finished on June 2, 1924.

British Enka Artificial Silk Company (later Courtauld's) took over the Aintree aircraft factory in 1925, and during the conversion, hundreds of unused and obsolete aircraft were disposed of. When the factory was officially opened by the Lord Mayor of Liverpool on October 22, 1926, the machinery was so secret that the Press was forbidden to take pictures inside the workrooms!

But Aintree's doyen factory was Hartley's, in Long Lane. This "village" factory employed about 1,200 for very many years. William Hartley, a native of Coln, first started making jam at Bootle in 1874, and after 12 years he opened a huge factory at Aintree, letting out houses on the hire-purchase principle. This was similar to Lord Leverhulme's project at

Aerial view of Hartley's factory, with village to the right. Pictured in 1930.

Port Sunlight, although not quite as ambitious. Hartley was a pioneer in social service and introduced profit-sharing, pensions, health service and recreational facilities for his employees, not to mention giving huge sums of money to charity, particularly hospitals, for which he and his daughter became so well known. The Christiana Hartley Maternity

Hospital in Southport is named after his daughter, who succeeded him as chairman after his death in October, 1922.

After nearly a century, it is interesting to learn what was said about Hartley by the Board of Trade in its first report (presented to both Houses of Parliament) on profit-sharing, in 1891:

"The preserves factory of Mr. W. P. Hartley at Liverpool has always sought to maintain good relations with his workpeople. His factory is a model. All the arrangements of this establishment indicate an employer who has been anxious that his prosperity should redound to the wellbeing of his workpeople."

The Aintree factory also produced canned vegetables from 1933, in addition to jams, marmalade and jellies, which was a great fillip to the local farmers who grew vegetables for this purpose. Hartley's was finally taken over by Schweppes in 1959, in a £2 million deal, and when one of the Victorian buildings on the site was being dismantled in 1977, an eleventh-hour bid was made by conservationists, including Councillor Ron Gould, to save its four-face tower clock from being sent to America. "So far as I know, this did not go to America, but was simply demolished," said Councillor Gould.

Aintree's obsolete mortuary came in for some scathing criticism in the early 1930's from the South West Lancashire Coroner, Mr. (later Sir) Samuel Brighouse. Time and again he declared that this building, little more than an "outhouse" was an insanitary place and a disgrace and that Sefton Rural District Council should take its cue from the "model" mortuaries at Bootle and Warrington.

At an inquest in November 1932, police surgeon Dr. V. J. Glover and Mr. Brighouse made a public protest against the Aintree mortuary, saying it was more like a slaughterhouse. Dr. Glover said that he had to perform a post-mortem by oil-lamp and the mortuary walls were in a filthy condition. He had to leave his hat and coat at the police station and walk to the mortuary in his shirt sleeves.

"When the mortuary is washed out, some of the blood and filth goes on to the grass," he said, warning of infection. "It is an insult to the human body — one of God's masterpieces — to put it in such a place."

The following year, in August, a Wigan pathologist said: "This shed, or outhouse, is the Gilbertian dream of a pathologist's hell."

Sixteen months later, the Coroner (now Sir Samuel Brighouse), still demanding council action, stated: "If my good wife had been found dead in this district and she had been placed in this dirty, disreputable outhouse in Aintree, with a dirty sheet over her, and I had to come and see her, I would have walked out and I should have cursed everyone. This place must be closed . . ." And close it did, bodies later being received at the more wholesome Ormskirk mortuary.

One of Aintree's oldest pubs (now completely rebuilt) was the original Blue Anchor Inn in School Lane, where horse-drawn coaches once drew up. In its pre-Great War brochure (when Mr. Legh Richman, of German descent, was the proprietor) it used to boast that it was "The Pride of Lancashire." Among its facilities were "a rustic bridge, rose, flower and tea gardens, and rustic stand to view the Grand National at the rear."

For many years an ancient, wheelless horse-drawn tramcar stood in this garden. One may still see the National course from the back of this inn, the bowling green of which borders the Leeds and Liverpool Canal. Through the inn's serene "backyard" once passed horse-drawn barges, laden with Lancashire's "lifeblood" in coal, cotton, machinery, grain and sugar.

Hounds used to be kept in kennels off nearby Bull Bridge Lane, where there was hunting thereabouts before and after the turn of the century. There also used to be a cock-pit in Melling Road.

Aintree was incorporated with Liverpool in 1905.

Just over Aintree's border and lying between Kirkby and Maghull is *Melling*, as yet comparatively unspoiled by the march of the city. Here, on a rocky hill, which rises from farmland once part of the marshes of ancient Warbreck Moor, stands the picturesque Parish Church of St. Thomas.

Although there was a chapel on this site in 1190, and possibly long before then, the hilltop is thought to have been a pagan burial ground since time immemorial. In 1319, when the cemetery was said to have been "polluted with blood" — after some unrecorded crime — it was discovered that the churchyard had never been consecrated.

Across the road from the church is the refurbished old inn, the Bootle Arms, whose sign bears the coat of arms of the Bootle family. The Bootles were one of the three chief farming families who settled in the district many centuries ago. The other two families were the Tatlocks and the Molyneuxes. Cromwell and some of his men are said to have stopped at this inn for a meal in 1643, when on their march to battle at Preston.

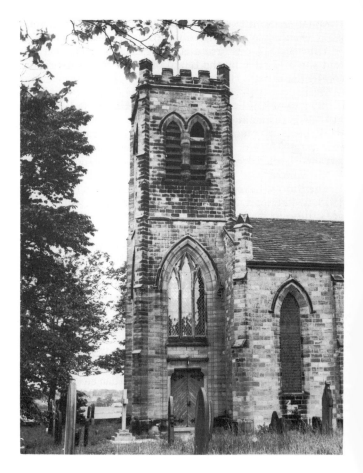

Melling Church, built in the 1830's on the site of 12th Century Melling Chapel.

Melling, incidentally — the haunt of highwaymen for many years, and the scene of some of their hangings — takes its name from the Old English "Mellingas," meaning "the followers of Mealla," who settled his little tribe there in the 6th Century.

Fazakerley, incorporated with Liverpool in 1904, has the distinction of being the only place so named in England. But its origin is a bit vague. The old Fazakerley family once lived there, but they took their name from the established district name, thought to be Anglo-Saxon, which could imply "meadowland, with a border or boundary field."

In 1379, Thomas de Fazakerleigh was County Coroner — an office which held considerable power in those days. About 1400, his successor, Robert, married Helen, heiress of Robert de Walton. Through their marriage some of the vast de Walton estates, including Spellowe House, passed into their family. John de Fazakerley was Mayor of Liverpool in 1428; Roger de Fazakerley was Mayor in 1531, and Samuel Fazakerley was Town Clerk from 1664 to 1678. Nicholas Fazakerley married the daughter of Colonel John Moore, of Bank Hall, the Parliamentarian who opposed Prince Rupert in the Civil War siege of Liverpool. Her mother was the daughter of Sir Richard Molyneux (of the family which produced the Earls of Sefton).

Fazakerley's famous "institution" for many years was its Cottage Homes, in Longmoor Lane, built in 1887-89 and now "listed." These originally comprised 21 cottage blocks (accommodating 584), with garden surroundings and a playing field, for the benefit of deprived children, cared for by foster-parents in charge of each unit. The Health Department acquired the homes in 1958 and converted the site into a mental health centre. In 1960, this became know as New Hall, Britain's largest training centre for mentally-handicapped people, with residential accommodation and including workshops, occupational-therapy unit, and so on.

For many years, until the Homes closed in 1958, an ornate pillar-box, about 3ft. 6in. high, was installed there for the benefit of the children. This was neither made nor placed by the Post Office but by the Cottage Homes' Board of Guardians, who paid a small fee to the Post Office for the collections it made. After the Homes closed, the Post Office rescued the box and, on asking in its house magazine if any other children's home would like this, was embarrassed by the number of replies. So, instead, the box was dispatched to the Merseyside County Museums and is now displayed in the Transport Gallery. To alleviate the disappointment of the applicants, the Post Office had toy replicas of the box made, filled these with sweets and sent them to the homes.

Like Aintree, Fazakerley was also linked with airmen in that 3611 (West Lancashire) Squadron Fighter Control Unit was stationed there. This unit ceased to operate in November, 1957, and was stood down on January 12, 1958.

At the Air Ministry's meteorological station in Field Lane, information from conditions of the upper atmosphere was provided by equipment carried by huge balloons, released several times a day. These assisted in the compilation of weather reports broadcast throughout the world.

In February, 1971, a large portion of the old 74-acre R.A.F. site was bought for housing development.

EVERTON & ANFIELD

LONG before Everton and Anfield were world-renowned for their famous football clubs, they were probably better known locally, anyway, for their cattle-grazing pastures. These had names like Hangfield (from which Anfield got its name), Whitefield and Netherfield, so familiar to us today. Hangfields were sloping fields, and even up to early in the last century certain fields in Walton were called "Hanging fields." Once upon a time, the farmers and small holders of Kirkdale would pay the township of Everton 6s 8d a year for cattle-grazing rights on the Everton pastures.

Everton — virtually "the heights of Liverpool" — developed a great reputation for its healthy geographical position, assailed by the pure sea air and also for the magnificent views it afforded of Merseyside, Deeside, North Wales and Liverpool Bay. And, of course, the ships, spreading their white canvas as they put to sea on their frequently perilous voyages. Many of the gentry built their large houses on its slopes and crest, the latter once nicknamed "Dunnock Brow" from its brown appearance.

The wealth, stability and position of these inhabitants earned them the name of "Everton nobles" — indeed, this area was the "Nob Hill" of Liverpool!

Even in the 13th Century, Everton was recorded as being a township, with "tenants . . . holding their lands by yearly rent and service to the King." It was then, of course, within the parish of Walton-on-the-Hill.

When part of the barony of Roger de Poictiers, the Conqueror's cousin, Everton appears in Domesday as Hiretun. But some historians think that this name really belongs to Tarleton and that Everton was but one of six unspecified berewicks pertaining to the Manor of Derbei (West Derby).

The earliest recorded mention of the district appears to be in a 1225 document of Henry III (where it is spelled as it is today). And, according to at least one scholar, Everton is composed of the Saxon transformation of the Celtic-Roman Eboracium or Evoracum into Eofor or Efer (meaning wild boar, and a common Saxon first-name), to which was added "wic," meaning village, or habitation. Thus, we get Efer's or Eorfor's farmstead . . . Hightown or Efer's farm? Take your pick!

The original village ran from the corner of Eastbourne Street, on the brow, in a curved line to the corner of Breck Road. Farmland lay about it and, in summer, with its cornfields, singing larks and scented May blossom, this was one of the fairest villages of Merseyside.

Up to the early 19th Century, the Fire Beacon was the oldest relic of the district, around which, on its grassy slope, hundreds of townsfolk would picnic on fine days. Built probably in mediaeval times, this stood six yards square and 25 feet high in about the position of the east corner of St. George's Church. Early in the reign of Charles I, some folk used to climb up to the beacon to be married there during the proscription of the clergy. When the Frenchman, Thurot's attack on Liverpool was anticipated in 1760, thousands gathered on this hill by the beacon to watch the estuary. Soldiers had orders to light the beacon as a warning if the

Everton Village, as it looked in about 1800. The little Round House (centre) still exists. The first house above the haystack incorporated the famous Everton Toffee shop; Prince Rupert's Cottage can be dimly seen, top right, and in its garden are arches made from whalebones, found on that site.

French fleet was sighted. Barrels of pitch and turpentine were kept in the upper chamber of this beacon, spared eventual demolition by collapsing one stormy night in 1803.

Incidentally, it was to a Liverpool man, Master Humfraye Brook, that Queen Elizabeth was indebted for the first news of the Armada's being at sea. A captain and shipowner, Brook, on passage from Liverpool to the Canaries, spotted the flotilla on its way to England. He hastened back to England and dispatched couriers with his report.

Up to 1815, there was a semaphore station on Everton hill. This was abandoned after the Battle of Waterloo.

Prince Rupert's Cottage, his headquarters during the Royalist siege of Liverpool in the Civil War, stood, until 1845,

at the west end of Everton Brow, (on the site of Eastbourne Street) overlooking the Valley. It was from these heights that Rupert surveyed Liverpool's mudwalled defences and made his historical comment that the town was but a crow's nest that a parcel of boys could take. So many souvenir pieces of wood were cut from the cottage's ancient timbers that it probably would have fallen down had it not been demolished in 1845!

Everton Beacon, Liverpool's earliest seafarers' navigational guide.

Two skeletons found in St. George's Churchyard early in the last century, were those of soldiers who had fought for Rupert and were interred there during the siege.

Nearby, in one of the small houses built in about 1692, Molly Bushell established her little "toffey" shop in 1753. Her toffee — the recipe of a Dr. Gerrard — was so delicious that those who had tasted it spread the good news far and wide. Queen Victoria and the Royal Family, not to mention celebrities like Dickens, enjoyed Everton toffee — not that made by Molly's fair hands, but certainly from her recipe. Everton Mints now seem to have taken over!

Archery was a popular summertime sport in old Everton and there were a number of competitive associations. In later years, many a wager was laid on winter curling competitions, too, when the local mere obligingly froze hard enough for these events. By the brink of the latter stood the "Mere Stones" and several more large stones like these marked Everton's ancient boundaries.

Sleeper's Hill derived its name from two parts of the commonland called the Great and the Little Sleeper. These eventually were enclosed as a seven-acre field and nicknamed Cobbler's Close by the shoemaker who bought the land. Later, Thomas Barton bought this ground and renamed it "Pilgrim," after making a fortune through the capture of a French ship by the English vessel of that name. This house was later renamed "Bronte." (See Kirkdale).

An ancient cross (later converted into a sundial) stood on Everton's Village Green as a four-foot, round pillar on three square stone steps. Here, in the days of yore when the "sweating sickness" was about, townspeople buying produce from the Everton farmers would place their coins in bowls of water. Plagues struck Liverpool many times over the centuries.

The sundial caused accidents when traffic bumped into it on dark nights and, one stormy night in 1820, a party of men led by Sir William Shaw, a surveyor, removed it completely and stored it in the old Round House. The first reaction of many villagers next morning was that the Devil had carried it off!

Sensational stories soon spread throughout the town and the truth was not generally known for many years.

Everton's Round House, sometimes called the "Stone Jug," was built in 1787 as a small lock-up, rather like the one on Wavertree's Village Green, and is still a landmark on the triangular piece of ground on Everton Brow. The small area around it was once used as a pinfold for sheep.

The junction of Rupert Lane, Breck Road (formerly sandy Breck Lane, leading to Club Moor and Gill Moss), Heyworth Street and Everton Road, was once called "Four Lane Ends" and here, in about 1680, a man who committed suicide after murdering his wife, was buried with a stake through his middle. The spiking was to prevent his body from being carried away by the "foul fiend."

A similar burial is said to have taken place at the top of Hatton Garden, Liverpool. This unsavoury custom was finally abolished by an Act of Parliament in 1825.

From the grounds of the Pilgrim Villa, to which I have referred, on August 12, 1812, Britain's earliest airman, James Sadler, made an ascent by balloon. A crowd of about 70,000 came to watch this as Sadler was then well known, having made his first ascent at Oxford in 1784. Many paid to stand within three reserved enclosures and saw him lift off shortly before 3 p.m., while the band from the Liverpool Guardship, H.M.S. Princess, played merrily. Considerably fewer, however, saw him land in West Derby village, having travelled a much shorter distance than expected.

The following October, Sadler attempted to cross the Irish Sea from Dublin to England by balloon. He nearly made it, but as darkness gathered and he was still way out over Liverpool Bay, off the North Wales coast, he decided to drop down to attract a ship, which would take him on board.

Unfortunately, the balloon dropped into the water and Sadler was dragged through the sea, half-drowned, before being picked up by a Manx fishing vessel, which eventually transferred him to the warmth and comfort of the guardship, Princess, anchored in the Mersey.

Sadler's son, William Windham Sadler, a balloonist like his father, was appointed engineer to Liverpool's first gas company, in Dale Street, in 1816. The following year, he succeeded where his father had failed by becoming the first man ever to cross the Irish Sea by air from Dublin to Liverpool.

Like many famous air pioneers in an age yet to come, William challenged fate once too often and, in September, 1824, he died in a fall from his balloon, near Accrington, during an attempt to float to Liverpool.

His remains were interred at Christ Church, Liverpool, demolished as derelict in 1927. The church's fenced-off graveyard, containing 1,400 bodies (exhumed and cremated in 1967), had caused public criticism ever since 1933, when children were found there playing cricket with a human skull for a ball, a shinbone for a bat and two leg bones for wickets!

Most famous of the handsome Everton villas was St. Domingo House, which had a varied career and left its name to streets and the large ward. This stood on part of 53 acres of commonland, purchased in 1757 by the wealthy West Indies merchant, Mr. George Campbell. It stretched from the top of the hill by St. George's Church to the Netherfield on one side and to the Breckfield on the other side.

He named the house after the incident involving the capture of a rich French prize by one of his ships, off the island of St. Domingo. Campbell died in 1770 and, three years later, his estate passed into the ownership of John Sparling, who had been Mayor of Liverpool in that year. A man of great wealth, Sparling demolished the old house and constructed " a noble residence," which stood there for about 150 years. He also had a tomb built at Walton Church so that this was visible from the house. Perhaps his idea was that successive generations of the family could not forget him!

When Sparling died, in 1800, the mansion went to his son, William, an officer in the Dragoon Guards. William was earmarked for a niche in local history because he was a participant in the next-to-last duel to be fought in Liverpool (See Toxteth). He left Merseyside after this duel and never returned. At his death, the restrictions on the St. Domingo estate were cancelled by an Act of Parliament and it was purchased by Mr. Ewart for £20,295.

During Sparling's absence abroad, the house was occupied by Prince William (later Duke) of Gloucester as Commander of Forces, Liverpool and District. Many jolly soirees were held there, attended by the Liverpool socialites who were almost intoxicated by having Royalty among their acquaintances. (In his quieter moments, it was said, the Prince sought the company of a young widow who lived in Gloucester Place, near St. Domingo House.)

Unfortunately, the Duke was slighted at one of the Town Hall mayoral banquets, due to the interference of his cousin, the Prince of Wales, also in attendance. Apparently the Duke felt that some of the honours to which he was entitled had been ignored and he withdrew. For the remainder of his stay in Liverpool his social relations with the town were considerably restrained.

In 1812, the government bought the estate from Mr. Ewart for military purposes, but after considerable local protest, this plan never materialised and the land was divided and sold. However, a large mansion in Rupert Lane, built in 1791 and originally owned by William Harper (Mayor in 1804), was converted into a cavalry barracks in September, 1848, and in 1854 Everton again became a military post, with several regiments successively occupying some of the big mansions there.

Now occupying but a mediocre plot, St. Domingo House became a girls' school and, 14 years later, a boys' school, patronised by the Unitarians. Two famous pupils of this school were William Rathbone and John Aloysius Smith, who became the author of "Trader Horn." In 1841, the house was purchased by the then Vicar-General, Dr. Youens, for the education of Catholic youths, and it opened the following year as St. Edward's College.

For nearly eight years part of its work was the preparation of students for the priesthood. Bishops Goss and O'Reilly and Archbishop Whiteside, spent many years there. When this side of the building's activities were transferred to Upholland in 1920, St. Edward's passed into the charge of the Christian Brothers. Then, shortly before the last war, the college removed to Sandfield Park, West Derby, and the Corporation acquired the old building site for housing.

The site of St. Domingo was once proposed for a cathedral and the plan went as far as building one of the chapels. When the project was abandoned, the chapel became the Parish Church.

St. Domingo Pit was a plot of land bounded by Breckfield Road North and Mere Lane, Everton, which for years was the scene of George Wise's Protestant open-air propaganda meetings. When this site became inadequate for public meetings of this kind, the Corporation, in 1910, allocated St. Domingo Recreation Ground, flanked on each side by playgrounds for girls and boys, and immediately adjacent to the Pit.

The enterprising developer of New Brighton, James Atherton, bought some of the broken-up St. Domingo estate and built a number of small streets of houses on this. From his own fine villa on the crest of Everton Hill, he weighed up the lovely vista of the Wirral and, having envisaged a resort among the sandhills and rocks at the end of the peninsular, spent the last years of his life constructing this.

Thomas De Quincey lived in Everton for some time, firstly with his mother and family, in the summer of 1801, at the

The cottage in which De Quincey once lived.

"tiny but sweet" cottage of Mrs. Best in Middle Lane (altered in 1817 to Everton Terrace). This one-storey, yellow-limed house was approached by a green wicket-gate and two stone steps. Everton Village then had only 87 houses and 499 inhabitants. After running away from Manchester Grammar School the following spring (1802), De Quincey again stayed in Everton — alone — and then, the next year, he was sent back to Everton from Chester by his mother, to be cared for by a family connection — a merchant named Craggs.

During his sojourn at Everton, De Quincey — best known for his "Confessions of an English Opium-Eater" — was befriended by William Clarke, Junior, a Liverpool banker, who lived in a mansion opposite the cottage.

Clarke treated the Manchester-born lad very kindly and even invited him to dine with local celebrities including William Roscoe, Dr. Currie (Burns' biographer) and Dr. William Shepherd, the minister of the Presbyterian (Unitarian) Chapel at Gateacre. These men were intimate friends who had formed "The Liverpool Literary Coterie."

When in Edinburgh, De Quincey published his "Literary Reminiscences" in Tait's Magazine. This included some unkind references to his old friends and soured his former relationship with the group.

In "Liverpool Banks and Bankers", John Hughes refers to the friends, " whose hospitality, as an unlicked cub of 16, De Quincey enjoyed, and on whose memory he, after years of debauchery had dulled his moral feelings, scattered the venom of ingratitude." De Quincey, of course, was a drug-addict.

After De Quincey's remarks, Shepherd, by then the sole survivor among the friends, published a scathing denial in the same magazine. The Liverpool newspapers of that day joined him in the chorus of abuse.

While at Everton in 1802, De Quincey recorded one of the biggest fires that Liverpool had experienced prior to the last-war bombing. This happened when some cotton warehouses in Goree Piazzas caught alight. De Quincey said that sparks from the blaze were blown as far as Warrington.

Horse-trams and private buses, run by Mason's in the later part of the last century, used to start from Holding's public house, on the corner of Holding Street, Everton. These went to town via Belmont Road, Whitefield road, West Derby Road, Farnworth Street, Kensington and London Road.

Like a number of Liverpool town districts, Everton had its own share of unmapped tunnels. The most interesting one to be discovered there and said to have been called "Prince Rupert's Tunnel," led from the cellars of an old house in Everton Road towards the river. The house, incorporating a much older, former country residence, and later considerably extended, was once known as "The Newsboys' Home," and the "Home of the Friendless and Destitute Boys," where young lads could get supper and a bed for the night. Shortly after the Great War the house was converted into a Y.M.C.A. Red Triangle Club, where some famous Liverpool sportsmen trained in their early years. It was demolished during the redevelopment of Everton after the last war.

In Granton Road, also before the end of the last century, there was a clock and watchmaker's shop, with a display-window full of working, mechanical models, which attracted scores of youngsters in the district. Next door was Pagendam's stables. John Pagendam was the coach proprietor who conveyed the Everton Football Team through the city to their ground from Lime Street Station in 1906, when they won the English Cup at Crystal Palace by beating

13

Newcastle United 1-0. His brother, Fred, also often conveyed Liverpool F.C.'s equipment in his wagonette.

A deep, sandstone quarry once stretched from Granton Road to Donaldson Street. A similar quarry also existed in Douglas Road, near Anfield Road Board School. And where the famous Anfield Kop now stands, there used to be a piece of land on which fairs and circuses were held.

The Kop end of Liverpool F.C's ground at the junction of Walton Breck Road with Kemlyn Road, pictured early this century. Note the great exit-gates and the steep steps to the terraces. Price of admission was sixpence (2½p) and, from half-time, 3d. Some of the boys in the picture wear suits and Eton collars; two more are bare-footed. The flag-post (upper right) was a mast that belonged to the Great Eastern, Brunel's giant, six-masted iron steamer, broken up at New Ferry about 1890.

Everton Football Club, formed in 1878 as St. Domingo Sunday Football Club and reformed the following year as Everton F.C., used to play on Liverpool's football ground at Anfield until 1892, when Everton bought Goodison Park for £8,600 after a dispute over rent with landlord Mr. John Houlding.

A meeting of shareholders was held at Houlding's hotel on March 15, 1892, and Liverpool F.C. was formed. Liverpool then took over Anfield Road. Goodison Park — former wasteland, cleared by volunteer supporters and the team — was opened on August 24 that year by Lord Kinnaird, President of the Football Association.

The original great flagpole at Liverpool's ground was the topmast of the old Great Eastern liner and was transported there from Garston on two wagons, hauled by three horses.

Another once well-known Anfield sports centre was the baseball ground in Lower Breck Road. This became the White City Greyhound Stadium, opened in August, 1932, and closed on October 6, 1973.

Anfield Cemetery, which lies between the two football grounds, had its first interment on May 5, 1863. It contains a magnificent memorial to the 3,966 citizens killed in air raids on Merseyside in the last war and covers a communal grave of 554 persons — 373 still unidentified. At the unveiling ceremony on May 8, 1951, ten years after the notorious "May Blitz," the Lord Mayor of Liverpool, Ald. The Rev. H. D. Longbottom said: "Liverpool was Port Number One in the war, and I doubt if any city was more severely bombed. To live here then was to live in the danger zone, one might almost say on the battle-front, and it is right and fitting that there should be an abiding monument to the Unknown Civilian, who died for his country in much the same manner as the

The Lord Mayor of Liverpool (Ald. the Rev. H. D. Longbottom) at the 1951 unveiling of a civic memorial to city victims of the 1941 "blitz" at Anfield Cemetery.

Unknown Soldier." Another shrine at Anfield Cemetery is that erected in 1950 to the memory of all Chinese domiciled in this country who have died here.

Few Merseysiders, however, realise that four blocks of catacombs, after the style of those in Rome, lie some 25 feet beneath Anfield Cemetery. These are lined on each side with deep stone recesses, but relatively few interments have been made there. A story connected with these catacombs is told about the Russian nobleman, whose wife died while they were visiting Liverpool. He had an expensive coffin made for her and "temporarily" deposited her remains in the Anfield catacombs with the avowed intention of building a church to

her memory and in which her body would be interred. However, soon after reaching his native land, he married again, found life blissful and obviously ignored his promise to his first wife, whose coffin lay in the catacombs for some years before being finally sealed up in one of the recesses.

About 1958, another man brought the remains of his wife, in a sealed coffin, all the way from South Africa to Anfield Cemetery. This was the last interment in the catacombs, which are still available for burials but now accommodating fewer than a score of coffins. Many once well-known people are interred at Anfield. Jem Mace, "last of the bare-knuckle fighters," who died at Barrow-in-Furness in 1910, is one. Only a 10in. × 5in. stone, numbered 595, in Church of England section No. 12, marks his lonely grave.

Stanley Park, also between the football grounds, was a delightful, well-patronised open space and is still well maintained in spite of Liverpool's post-war tide of vandalism. This was bought piecemeal from various small landowners between 1866-69, at a total cost of £177,474.

It cost £49,213 to lay out the area as a park, which has always been popular and welcome in this area of the city, not so rich in open spaces as the south side. On its fine terrace, backed by a splendid carved sandstone wall, with recessed arches and pillared shelters, there was a grand view to be had. At intervals along this walk stood telescope stands, and visitors with those, on a clear day, could not only see the estuary, but prominent points like Black Combe in Cumberland, Snaefell in the Isle of Man, Ashurst Beacon and Longridge Fell.

Before the park was opened in May, 1870, and for some years afterwards, its boundary at the end of the terrace was old Mill Lane, a country road running between hedges and rush-grown ditches. When eventually encompassed by the encroaching park, this lane became a leafy pathway running through the heart of the estate.

An outdoor bathing-pool there was opened in 1923 and gave endless pleasure to youngsters on warm summer days until its closure 40 years later. Stanley Park's Palm House — presented by Mr. Henry Yates Thompson (who also gave Sefton Park Palm House to the city), was opened in 1899. This was his memorial to Liverpool's W. E. Gladstone, four times Prime Minister. It was badly damaged by bomb blast in the last war and not reopened until September 15, 1958.

Part of the "Pageant of Cuckooland," which took place in Stanley Park in 1929.

Adding to this pleasant retreat, with its boating-lake, sheltered glen and rustic bridges, were a paddling-pool, a children's garden with floral cuckoo clock, wishing well and a plethora of ornamental wild creatures and fairytale characters.

These and other gifts were presented to the park in 1929 by wealthy businessman, patron of the arts and benefactor, Mr. George Audley, of Lulworth Road, Birkdale, who, in 1927, had also given the bronze Peter Pan statue to Sefton Park.

A special "Pageant of Cuckooland," in which 1,200 schoolchildren took part, in addition to a cast of 60, was held in Stanley Park to celebrate this event on September 21, 1929. It was repeated at the Hippodrome Theatre as a free show for 2,400 poor kiddies by the kindly Mr. Audley, on November 2. The Children's Garden took the place of an aviary, dismantled because it was too exposed to cold winds. To celebrate the park's centenary in 1970, a giant cake, baked in 16 parts, fitted together, iced and weighing nearly 500 lbs, was designed as a detailed model of the park, with bandstand, boating lake and all.

George Audley, a bachelor who loved children, and who "showered gifts on his native city," also gave Sefton Park its famous Eros monument — a replica of that in London's Piccadilly. Sadly, he died suddenly in February, 1932, only a few months before the statue was installed.

SEAFORTH & LITHERLAND

ALTHOUGH virtually part of ancient Litherland, named by the Vikings and meaning "sloping land," the Seaforth district took its name from a Scottish laird. At a time when wealthy Liverpool businessmen were seeking salubrious and attractive areas of Merseyside for their residences, merchant Sir John Gladstone, M.P., had a house built near the shore at Litherland and he removed there in 1813.

Sir John's wife was a Scot, belonging to the Mackenzie Clan, the head of which was Lord Seaforth. They named their house after him and that is how Seaforth district became known as such. This house, long-gone, was a big square mansion with a first-floor gallery around the hall. House and grounds stood in the part now defined by Elm Road (where the entrance was), Rawson Road, Gordon Road and Gladstone Road,

Another famous residence of the district was Seaforth Hall, the estate of which was bought by the Mersey Docks and Harbour Board on October 8, 1903, for dock extensions. The house itself was demolished in 1924 for the extension of Gladstone Dock (named after Robert Gladstone, a chairman of the Dock Board).

The hall's foundation stone, laid by Mrs. James Muspratt on May 2, 1839, contained current coins of the realm This was a lovely mansion, designed in Greek style by Liverpool architect and historian, Sir James Picton, for James Muspratt, the "father" of the alkali industry in Lancashire, who decided to build himself "a house of noble dimensions and classic style."

In Muspratt's day, it was known as the most hospitable mansion in Liverpool, and people like Dickens, Sheridan, Knowles and Macready were visitors there. Dr. E. K. Muspratt, who died in 1923, was its last occupant.

However, the Seaforth residence which commanded most public attention was Seafield House. This was the home of shipping merchant William James Fernie until April, 1880, when he and others formed the International Marine Hydro Company and the house and its six-storey northern wing were converted into a luxurious, 250 bedroomed hotel, within 10 acres of ground.

The hotel, with facilities for tennis, bowls, quoits, archery, boating, and also boasting a gymnasium and a conservatory, was designed to capture overnight travellers using the busy transatlantic liner services. Its grand opening, by the Earl of Lathom, took place on September 25, 1882. But, alas, the travellers turned out to be birds of passage, who did not linger in the port. And there was inadequate transport from the docks to Seaforth. So the venture failed. The hotel became known as "Fernie's Folly."

From July 4, 1884, the building was used as a convent and school run by the Institute of the Sacred Heart of Mary. The rich furnishings gave way to simple refectory tables and desks. The Dock Board started negotiating for the property in 1905, with an eye to extending the north docks. Three years later, the convent and school removed to Crosby Road.

Seafield House remained empty until 1912, when the Lancashire Asylums Board took it over and, in 1913, the Suffragettes set it on fire, causing £80,000 worth of damage.

Seaforth sands were always popular with the Liverpool townfolk. Modern swimsuits would have been taboo in this Victorian scene, but even if sunlight could not reach these young bodies, all at least benefited from the fresh sea air. Top right: Muspratt's Seaforth Hall and estate. (Crosby Library).

Seafield House, reduced from its former six stories, pictured in 1967 after the Inland Revenue removed to Bootle.

Two storeys were destroyed, reducing the building to four storeys. The north wing was rebuilt and the building was then used as a home for mentally-retarded children, until these were evacuated just before the last war.

It then became a naval hospital for the Battle of the Atlantic casualties from March, 1941, until 1947, when the Admiralty gave it up. In May, 1950, the Inland Revenue, removing from Llandudno, occupied it. Seafield House was scheduled for demolition in September, 1967, when the Royal Seaforth Dock's project got under way.

Liverpool was the first port in the world to introduce a port-radar system and this was pioneered from a dockside hut in 1948. Today, in the north-west corner of the Royal Seaforth Dock, is a modern radar station, which provides a round-the-clock navigational service for ships.

Seaforth Coast Radio Station, which closed on May 14, 1960, and transferred to its present station at Nebo, Amlwch, Anglesey, began its ship-to-shore (and vice-versa) communications system in 1903. A primitive building, with corrugated-iron roof and built on Seaforth sands, this was known as the "Tin Tabernacle" and was run by Marconi, combining the functions of service depot, training school and coast radio station.

In September, 1909, when the Government decided to take a hand in radio communication and assume responsibility for safety services, the station was taken over by the Post Office. That year, Seaforth Radio provided radiotelegraph (Morse code) communications with ships using the Mersey ports, or on passage in the Irish Sea, and with ships plying to and from Ireland and the Isle of Man. However, when radiotelephony equipment was first developed for the smaller ships in the early 1930's, the possibility of connecting them to the telephone subscribers on shore was pioneered and first exploited in the Liverpool area.

The Mersey Docks and Harbour Board was Seaforth's oldest and largest radiotelephone customer and the Board's pilot boat was selected to take part in tests made as early as November/December, 1933, by which it was able to prove that connection between a ship's radiotelephone apparatus and the inland telephone system was a practical proposition. A more permanent home for this historical station was found in the grounds of the military barracks at Seaforth.

Seaforth Barracks — accommodating once famous and colourful regiments, like the King's Royal Dragoons, the Royal Field Artillery, Liverpool's own King's Regiment, the Scots Greys and the Hussars — was the scene of rioting at the outbreak of the Great War in August, 1914. Hundreds of people representing the families of many soldiers within the barracks tried to force their way in to say goodbye before their loved ones departed for France.

Earlier, in the 1880's, the late Lord Baden-Powell, founder of the Scout Movement, was stationed in these barracks. He said that this was where his scouting days really began.

Baden-Powell did much of his training with arms here, particularly with the new machine-guns, which he fired in the nearby sandhills. His enthusiasm for this weapon is said to have resulted in his promotion and eventual postings to Africa, where he played such an important part in the defence of Mafeking.

Liverpool's first river fortifications were established at the "Nabbe beyond the Poole," (now the north end of Salthouse Dock) and a fort was also built at Seaforth in about 1880. This contained four huge guns, often used by the old Artillery Volunteers for practice. The battery took the place of the one

A pre-Great War military band emerging from Seaforth Barracks, built in 1882.

The King's birthday salute being fired from Seaforth Battery some years before construction of the Gladstone Dock system began.

19

at Huskisson Dock, erected by the Government in 1854, which superceded an even older and similar battery, which stood at the "Hog's Head Nook," on the site of the present Collingwood Dock.

Much later, and currently well within the living memory of many Merseysiders, was Seaforth's Greyhound Racing Stadium, in Crosby Road South, which opened in 1933 and closed in 1966. An earlier whippet-track was located in Sandy Road.

Of interest to railway enthusiasts, perhaps, is that the foundations of the old bridge, carrying the railway line over Seaforth Road, were built on bales of cotton, said to be the best substance to settle in sand. Seaforth Sands was the terminus of the world-renowned Liverpool Overhead Railway, running the full length (6½ miles) of the old Liverpool docks from Dingle. This was the first elevated electric railway in the world and the first British passenger escalator is said to have been operated at this station. Regrettably, the Overhead, so modern in concept so long ago, was demolished in 1956.

Litherland, close neighbour of Seaforth and Waterloo, and mentioned in the Domesday Book as Liderlant and Literland, is part of the area once split between the Saxon thanes Uctred and Elmae. The former owned considerable areas of Merseyside in his day. For centuries Litherland was rural and supported only by a farming community. Later, and for many years, it belonged to the powerful Molyneux family, who became the Earls of *Sefton*.

This latter district's name, incidentally, is a combination of the Old Norse "Sef" and the Old English "tun," probably meaning swampy land, with rushes and waterways, as undoubtedly it once was. Pre-war, flooded Sefton Meadows was a very popular place for ice-skaters in times of hard frost. North-eastwards, between Litherland and Warbreck Moor, was Stand Park, which once belonged to Sefton Hall, the earlier seat of the Earls of Sefton, who later resided at Croxteth Hall. The old estate was well stocked with deer and a handsome lodge within this area was recorded as being a ruin in 1773. Sefton Church is one of the oldest buildings in the county and a stone in its outside wall bears the date 1111.

The oldest recorded building in Litherland seems to be the black and white, four-bedroomed "Darwin Cottage," at 71 Sefton Road. The Darwins were well-known local farmers. This cottage was built in 1818 on the site of another, dated 1630, the datestone of which is preserved. It used to have a large orchard attached to it and adjoined Oak Farm.

One of the best-known occupants of Darwin Cottage, where he and his family lived for many years, was the late

"Darwin Cottage".

Sefton Church, founded in the 12th Century, but largely rebuilt in the reign of Henry VIII. (L. Turnock).

Deputy Chief Constable of Bootle, Superintendent Allan Crabtree Watson, former police prosecutor with an outstanding record of service, for which he received the M.B.E. and the King's Police Medal. A linguist, he often made use of his ability to speak French, Spanish, Russian and German, in the Bootle courts, where many foreign seamen appeared over the years. He retired in 1952 but stayed on at the cottage for many more years and finally died at Burley, Yorkshire, in October, 1974, aged 87.

Further down Sefton Road is relatively-modern Litherland Town Hall. The latter will always be associated with the Beatles, who made numerous appearances there. These were in the famous foursome's early days, when they were hardly known outside of Merseyside and performed for the now seemingly ludicrous fees of £8 and £15 a night!

St. Andrew's Church, Litherland, which suffered like so many other buildings in that area from the severe wartime bombing, had its hall destroyed. This was replaced by the new "Memorial Hall," honouring those churchworkers (members of the WVS) who were killed when caring for the homeless billeted in the hall.

Another house of worship in the district which attracted big congregations with its "Hot Gospel" approach, and where hymns were really sung with gusto, was Walker's Mission. Old Mrs. Walker, who founded the mission in a corrugated-iron hut (later rebuilt into a fine chapel), used to drive around in a brougham "like Queen Victoria."

Dreadful flooding, with water in some places as deep as 10 feet, used to occur in Litherland (and Bootle) before the Rimrose Brook Drainage Scheme sewer was opened in October, 1949. Property in Irving Street, Palmerston Avenue, Bridge Road and Garrick Street, particularly, were badly affected at times of heavy rainfall, when the sewers could not cope with the water. A cyclist was drowned in floodwater under the railway bridge in Akenside Street, Bootle, in 1934.

Litherland's first council school was opened in Lander Road in September, 1901, but its first church school, started in 1863, was in a room over stables at the Litherland Hotel. The latter continued until St. Philip's Church School was opened in January, 1867.

SPEKE & HALE

SPEKE (like Fazakerley) boasts a unique name in that its is the only one in England. Another honour for the city satellite town, in addition to its famous city airport, is that when planned it was described as a "model town for the whole country." The land was brought by Liverpool Corporation in 1929 and construction began in 1937.

Creator of Speke as a town was Sir Lancelot Keay, who died, aged 91, in November, 1974. Sir Lancelot was City Architect and Director of Housing in Liverpool from 1925 to 1948 and President of the Royal Institute of British Architects from 1946 to 1948. He was responsible for building more than 35,000 houses and flats. He took pains to see that many of Speke's historical and attractive geographical features were not overwhelmed in the plan and, today, the river area, including *Oglet* and the Hale end of the township, has been preserved as a green belt, with Speke Hall, particularly, standing as serene as ever in its own ancient grounds.

The land, which became the huge industrial, housing and airport area, cost £90 an acre. And yet two carucates of this region were worth only 64 pence a year when originally owned by Uctred, the Saxon thane, who held a number of Merseyside manors. The Domesday Book recorded the district as Speke and this possibly may be derived from the Anglo-Saxon "spec-hus" — a court hall. This would point to Speke Hall, but as the hall was not constructed for a couple of centuries later, the name probably came from the Anglo-Saxon "spic" (German, speck), signifying "bacon" and used to describe swine fields, of which Merseyside had many.

After Uctred, the manor passed down to Benedict de Gerneth, Lord of Espeake and Oglhal (Oglet), Adam de Molyneux (from whom the Earls of Sefton are descended), and then the Norreis family (also spelt Norreys, and finally Norris). The Norrises, a widely-spread family, were big landowners even in the 13th Century and the Norrises of Speke probably originated from the Formby branch of the family. They were associated with the Speke area for about five centuries.

Speke and the tiny hamlet of Oglet, together representing about 2,600 acres in 1811, then had but 37 houses occupied by 70 families all employed in agriculture, except for a wheelwright and a blacksmith.

Pride of Speke, and indeed the whole of Liverpool, is its magnificent old hall, a Grade 1 listed building and one of the finest examples of timber-framed building in Britain. Visitors to this large and delightful Elizabethan manor-house really do step back in time as they cross the bridged dry moat leading to the main entrance and cobbled inner courtyard.

One of the first lords in the long Norris line of succession, Thomas Norreys, who inherited the manor in 1467, compiled a list of all the family property, which covered a 14ft. 7½in. continuous roll of parchments stitched together. This was known as the Great Norreys Rental. There was also a separate scroll called the Garston Rental of the Abbot of Whalley Abbey. Pious Thomas endowed the chantry of St. Thomas the Martyr at Childwall (part of which is said to be incorporated in the Childwall Abbey Hotel).

Open farmland field ponds, near Clough Road, Speke – once an exciting but highly dangerous playground. Pictured in 1958.

One of the famous Norris family, Sir William Norris, an M.P. for Liverpool, who in 1702, bequeathed to the Corporation its first Sword of State.

His eldest son, William, knighted after fighting in the Battle of Stoke, founded Speke Hall, although much of the hall, as it appears today, was constructed by his grandson, also William, who became Lord of Speke when only 23. Having taken part in the Earl of Hertford's expedition to Scotland in 1540 and in the subsequent looting of Holyrood Palace, he returned with considerable booty to Speke Hall. A Bible amongst this eventually was presented to Liverpool's Athenaeum Library, via the Marquis of Salisbury. At the end of his military career, Sir William became Mayor of Liverpool in 1554 and an M.P. for the town.

The Norrises were a great martial family and strongly Royalist during the Civil War. They held their estate by military tenure, which they also imposed on their tenants. General Sir John Norris, when fighting a battle against Don John of Austria, in the 16th Century, had three horses killed under him in one day!

23

Sir William's grandson, also William and also knighted, probably hid and maintained priests at Speke Hall and in other places. He was openly accused of sending money and arms "to the King's enemies beyond the seas," and eventually became a convicted recusant. (See Childwall). Staunch Catholics though they had been, the Norrises, in 1650, accepted the new Church of England faith — at least ostensibly. Even so, William (who succeeded his father, the latter Sir William) directed that he be buried with his ancestors in the former Catholic Norris Chapel at Childwall.

The long line of direct-descent Norris tenants of Speke Hall ended with the death, in 1731, of Richard Norris, Mayor of Liverpool in 1700, and M.P. for the town from 1708 to 1710.

Lovely Speke Hall was fast decaying when Charles George Beauclerk inherited it, and some of the rooms were reduced to providing shelter for cattle. He leased the hall for 17 years, by the end of which it was nearly a ruin. Finally, in 1795, he sold the whole estate.

Richard Watt, a little merchant who made a fortune in the

Speke Hall, one of the finest Elizabethan buildings in Britain and a renowned Liverpool tourist attraction.

West Indies (see Old Swan) bought Speke Hall that year. His descendant, also Richard Watt, inherited the hall and when he died in 1865, this was kept in trust for his daughter, Adelaide, who took possession of it when she was 21. And there she stayed until she died in 1921, aged 64. She, too, left the estate in trust for some three members of the Norris family, named in her will, with her nephew, Mr. Hewson, for 21 years. At the end of this term he would benefit from it during his lifetime. As things turned out, Mr. Hewson arranged for the National Trust to take over the old hall and Liverpool City Council later leased this from the Trust for 99 years.

One of the last tenants of Speke Hall was Canon Edward Norris, Dean of Westminster Abbey, who stayed at the hall from time to time in the 1930's.

Although today we can reach Speke Hall by car and public transport with no difficulty, the hall was very much isolated from the city up to and even beyond the turn of the century. Shortly before Liverpool celebrated its 700th anniversary in 1907, with a massive summer pageant held on Wavertree Park adjoining Tournament Hall, Edge Lane, Miss Watt, then owner of Speke Hall, offered to open her home to visitors for six days. A notice about this in "The Pageant News" stated that the hall "is about two miles' walk from Speke Station . . ." However, this did not deter our forbears, who had no radio, television or cinemas to amuse them, and 3,000 visitors took up Miss Watt's kind offer!

One of France's earliest airmen, Matthew Vallet, of Juval, near Paris, lived in Liverpool during his later years and established a bleaching works at Garston. A daughter of his married a Mr. Grace, of Speke Hall, and Vallet died there at the age of 91.

Modern Speke is chiefly renowned for important Liverpool Airport, which is a vital link in the North West's air-traffic system. The site originally was selected in the late 1920's for the Corporation by pioneer airman (of flying-circus fame), Sir Alan Cobham. From a humble start, with a farmhouse acting as its flying-control building (pictured here), the airport today boasts first-rate passenger and cargo facilities and a huge, riverside runway, capable of serving the needs of the largest and fastest aircraft. Future plans include a new terminal, roads and car-parks, all based on a one-runway operation.

Speke village is now represented by a tiny, almost isolated area in Hale Road, containing All Saints' Church, consecrated in 1876, a small sandstone school, of about the same date, and a terrace of late 18th Century cottages. Before All Saints was built, local folk were buried at Childwall or at Walton. Oglet Lane, once an extension of Hale Road,

Water, woodland, sand and shingle made Oglet one of Merseyside's beauty spots and a favourite picnic place. The bay lies between Dungeon Point and Hale Lighthouse.

formerly led to Oglet and the river, but the airport runway now bisects this lane and the hamlet is reached via Dungeon Lane. Now almost cut off completely from Speke, Oglet is comprised of a couple of farms and a few cottages, but fishing and a modicum of boat-building used to be carried on there. It was also a famous local shrimping village, like Marshside at Southport, and Parkgate, Wirral. Seeing the Oglet women, with their baskets laden with shrimps, trudging to the Garston market was once a common sight.

Before the last war, there was much talk about a riverfront strip at Speke being safeguarded for part of a continuous promenade in future years. Certainly there is ample scope along Oglet's "countryside" bank for part of this. Similar thoughts prevail today about providing Hale also with a

paved riverside walk. Meanwhile, the nearest section of Promenade to Speke, on that stretch of coast between Hale and the Pier Head, is the short length of private prom at Cressington Park.

Tales of a four-mile long, under-river tunnel between Speke and Bebington, used by monks of long ago, and said to be haunted, might have some foundation in fact. For countless years there have been stories about three tunnels, which are supposed to have started at the ancient Birkenhead Priory, by Cammell Laird's shipyard. One of these ended at New Brighton's red rocks (the old "Red Noses"), another cut through to Stanlawe or Ince, and the third is supposed to have led towards the Mersey. Could the latter have been that which crossed to Speke or Garston, once part of the territory occupied by monks attached to Stanlawe Abbey?

Another legend tells how one of a number of monks from Birkenhead Priory was crushed by a boulder as they were making their way through a tunnel in an attempt to save the priory's valuable plate during a raid by Henry VIII's commissioners. The falling rubble entombed the remainder alive. Perhaps the incident gave rise to the "haunting" aspect of the Speke tunnel. If the tunnel ever existed, it must have been the first Mersey Tunnel!

Speke's close neighbour is the picturesque and well-preserved old village of *Hale*, which somehow has managed to retain so much of its rural architecture and environment although jammed in between the great industrial region of Widnes and Liverpool. Thomas Carlyle's wife, in 1844, went as far as to declare Hale as "the beautifullest village in all England." And, even today, its delightful "fairy-story" thatched cottages and gorgeous blooming bulb fields certainly make for a very colourful picture. The village became the heart of the biggest bulb-growing industry in the North West, supplying hundreds of thousands of blooms to the markets. Not surprisingly, one or two Dutch folk have settled there.

Unlike Speke, Hale (formerly an Anglo-Saxon settlement and given its Charter in 1203 — four years before Liverpool), carries a fairly common English place-name. This probably comes from the Anglo-Saxon word "heall," meaning a large house or hall, of which there was ample evidence in ancient Hale Hutte, seat of the Ireland family.

However romantic to speculate on this derivation, as Hale was referred to in the 13th Century as "the land of Hales," and "the town of Halis" (Old Norwegian healas or halas means "slopes"), the name was more likely to have signified "the slopes" — or fields slanting down towards the river.

Hale was given to Johannes de Hibernia, who arrived in Britain with William the Conqueror, and he built the first chapel-of-ease there in 1081. When he died, only seven years later, he was buried at the chapel, which came within the jurisdiction of the parish of Childwall. In 1203, King John granted all the manor (except for his hunting ground at *Halewood*) to Richard de Walton, son of Gilbert de Walton, Chief Sergeant of the West Derby Hundred. Richard was a great favourite of the King and was a priest who had accompanied him in Ireland in 1185. He was given the title of Richard de Mida (of Meath).

In 1221, Henry III confirmed this land grant to Richard and his heirs and about 1300, through Adam Austyn de Ireland, the manor passed down to the Irelands, a family whose name has been associated with the Hale, Halewood, Speke and Garston region for many centuries.

The village of Halewood in about 1910. To the right is the original Derby Arms, which stood on the site of the present hotel of that name. (Knowsley Libraries).

The well-known Fleetwood-Hesketh family eventually took possession of the Hale estates before the last war. Mr. Peter Fleetwood-Hesketh came to live at the Manor House (once known as the Parsonage House and overlooking the village green). Although not as grand a building as the then decaying Hale Hall had been, the Manor House is a brick and sandstone building with an impressive frontage and part of it is 17th Century. It was added to considerably by the Rev. William Langford in the early 18th Century. The building later became a farmhouse (Manor Farm) and the military occupied it for some time during the last war. Today, bereft of the ancient ivy which once veiled its handsome face, it presents a fitting residence for the "squire."

Hale Hutte, or the Haute, or the Old Hutt as it was latterly called, was a moated manor house on the site where Ford's factory now stands. It has been demolished only since the last war. The Yerlands, or Irelands, as they became known by, occupied the Hutte from about 1291. The Lords of Hale had many privileges. They could demand anchorage-money from the owners of ships sheltering on their coast; claim ownership of all "royal fish" (like sturgeon), and "wrecks and waifs of the sea within these waters."

William Davies painted this picture of the Old Hutte in 1850, when some of its out-buildings existed and its ancient moat still contained water.

The Hutte, which many folk can still remember as a farmhouse, adjoined what was once a massive 12th Century hall, the ruins of which stood nearby. This must have been a residence of considerable importance in its day. It stood out alone in the fields of Halewood between Hale and Hunts Cross before this area was redeveloped. A three-storey house, it stood on a square island, surrounded by a moat and once boasted a drawbridge. A stone in the building was carved with the armorial bearings of the Ireland and Hanford families. A scheme for its restoration was ordered by Liverpool City Council in 1952, with the object of converting it into a folk museum. Unfortunately, the building, riddled with dry-rot, was in too bad a state for this to be done.

Hale Hall, another fine old building, built by the first Sir Gilbert Ireland between 1617 and 1626 at Hale village and nearer to the river, was also sadly allowed to decay and was demolished only recently. This became the residence of the Ireland family (of the Hutte) and, later, of the Ireland Blackburn families. Colonel Sir Gilbert Ireland — born in 1624 and the most famous member of this family — considerably altered Hale Hall (built by his grandfather), in 1674, the year that he became Mayor of Liverpool.

Gilbert was quite a "power in the land." Among the honours bestown on him were High Sheriff of Lancashire, M.P. for Lancashire and Liverpool, and Constable of Liverpool. He was knighted by King Charles II. Gilbert died in 1675 from "apoplexy." He was only 51. His epitaph, on a slate tombstone in the chancel of Hale Church recorded that he was "the last of his house," and as the slab was ruined when the church was gutted by fire, a replica is to be made. The Irelands had held Hale since 1291.

Hale Hall, the estate of which is now a recreation park, was given a new southern frontage (similar to that on the north side) in 1806 by Mr. John Blackburne. This was designed by John Nash. Carved over the fireplace in a fine old oak-

St. Mary's Church before the disastrous fire.

panelled room at the hall were the arms of Aspinwall, Halsall, Ireland, Molyneux and Stanley — all famous Lancastrian land-owning families.

An unknown species of palm tree, said to have been the only one to have fruited in Europe and given the name of "Sabal Blackburnia," after John Blackburne's daughter, was cultivated among the many rare and exotic plants at Hale Hall in the 18th Century. The tree originally was presented to the family by Lord Petre in 1737, when they lived at Orford Hall, near Warrington. It was brought to Hale Hall in 1817 and lived until 1859. The palm, known as "The Great Palm of Hale," flowered annually and produced fruit like bunches of black grapes. Its trunk is preserved at Kew Museum.

Little is known about the chapel in Hale built by Johannes de Hibernia in 1081, but the second Church of St. Mary, built in the 14th Century of wattle and daub and with a sandstone tower, was taken down in 1758 and rebuilt. However, its ancient tower was not dismantled and this still stands today. The third church, with fine stained-glass windows, was a picturesque focal point in the village until October 19, 1977, when it was deliberately set on fire and gutted, leaving only its shell and the old tower (with one side badly scorched) standing. The villagers bravely decided to restore St. Mary's to its former glory and this they have done. The little church looks as lovely as ever on its ancient site.

Within the churchyard lies buried the fabulous Childe of Hale — a 9ft. 3in. giant named John Middleton. John, born in 1578 and of normal growth during his youth, became a national celebrity when he was 39. This happened because

King James I, en route to Scotland in 1617, spent a few days in Lancashire. While at Lathom, he knighted Gilbert Ireland (the earlier Sir Gilbert, of the Hutte, who built Hale Hall). The King, who had heard about Sir Gilbert's huge bodyguard, was fascinated by the giant and invited both master and servant to the court in London. Big John arrived — resplendent in colourful costume, with ruffs, buckles, bows and all. And he was soon challenged by the King's champion to a wrestling bout.

This bout, we are told, lasted a long time — until John, in throwing the champ, dislocated the latter's thumb and was declared the winner. The courtiers, who had backed the champion were not too happy about this! John was given a gift of some 20 guineas by the King and dispatched back to Hale with his master. And, it is said, while on this journey, thieves stole his purse and money. Poor John!

Sir Gilbert and John called at Oxford on the way home. Gilbert had matriculated at Brasenose College and, again, could not resist showing off while there by producing the biggest man in Britain. John left the impression of one of his hands on the doorpost of a cellar at the college. This was given a gilded background and remained there until about 1886.

It was this hand-impression which prompted diarist Samuel Pepys to record on June 9, 1668: "To Oxford, a very sweet place . . . After come home from the schools I went out with the landlord to Brazen-nose College:— to the butteries, and in the cellar find the hand of the Childe of Hales . . . long." The diarist omitted to give the measurement! But the dimensions of this giant are recorded thus: "From the carpus to the end of his middle finger was 17 inches long, his palm 8 inches and a half broad and his whole height 9 feet, 3 inches."

A similar hand-print is displayed today in the village pub

Giant John Middleton's grave, which lies in the churchyard at the rear.

"The Childe of Hale," reputed to be haunted — but not by Big John. A life-size portrait of John Middleton (there were more than one of these), which once hung in Hale Hall, was presented to Brasenose College in 1924 by Colonel Ireland Blackburne.

Giant John, a gentle soul in spite of his colossal strength (he was said to have thrown a bull to the ground), was really a man of the soil and he returned to farming at Hale to wander no more. He died in 1623, and when, in 1768, out of curiosity, his remains were exhumed from St. Mary's churchyard, his thigh bones alone were found to measure 2ft. 9 inches. John's remains were eventually re-interred in the churchyard, only a few yards from also lies his benefactor.

Big John's thatched cottage may still be seen in the village with its ceiling taken right up to the roof to allow for his height. His hat-pegs in the cottage were fixed about ten feet from the floor.

The notorious and historic Hale Ford led across a wide stretch of the Mersey between Hale and Weston. This began at the shore end of Within Way. Scores of people and animals have met their deaths walking this highly dangerous sandbank route, particularly in mist, which shrouds the deadly banks and deep channels of this huge and unpredictable river. Graves in Hale churchyard testify to at least a small percentage of those who died on this watery highway and were buried under epitaphs like "Traveller Unknown, Drowned." According to records of the manor, fisherman John Walley, of Runcorn, was drowned on the Eve of All Saint's Day, 1423, when trying to cross the river by this ford with two pack-horses carrying "Formby fish." The pack-horses managed to swim to safety but John and his own horse perished.

Soldiers often used this ford at the time of the Civil War and Prince Rupert and his Cavaliers, fighting in Lancashire, forced their prisoners, captured at Bolton and tied in pairs, to cross the ford on foot as the tide was rising. The prisoners only just made it because they had the sense to support each other. Rupert and his men also crossed the ford on their return to Cheshire after being routed at Marston Moor. Lord Francis Lovel, whose home was at Halewood, vainly tried to reach the Hale shore from the Cheshire side of the river after escaping from the Battle of Bosworth in 1485. He managed to ride to the Mersey at Ince but was drowned with his horse when crossing. His property eventually was handed over to the Earls of Derby.

Last of the Massey family, of ancient Puddington Hall in Wirral (there were three successive halls), William Massey joined the army of the "Old Pretender" and fought at the Battle of Preston. After the defeat of the Jacobite army there, he rode the 45 miles from Preston to Puddington, fording the Mersey at Hale. This murderous, uninterrupted ride was tough enough on the 60-years-old rider, but it killed his poor horse. It fell dead outside its stable and was buried on the spot.

Another escaping soldier, Lord Molyneux, routed at Kirkham by Roundhead Colonel Ashton, fled across this ford into Cheshire.

The ford was in use up to about the middle of the last century, when horses and carts were still being driven across. A minister at Hale, the Rev. Thomas Blackburne, in 1808, removed to his new parish at Wrexham by crossing Hale Ford — taking all his possessions with him.

Hale Lighthouse, at Hale Head, the most southerly edge of "old" Lancashire (Hale is now within Cheshire), made

Hale Lighthouse used to be the most southern point of Lancashire. Made redundant by the Upper Mersey Navigation Commissioners in 1958, it is now a private residence. Its rocky shore has always been a favourite picnic spot.

redundant in May, 1958, when shipping traffic on the Upper Mersey was sadly diminished, is now a picturesque private residence. The original lighthouse was built in 1836, and the last one — a taller structure — in 1906. The old keeper's cottage, demolished when the property was bought for private use, had been built long ago as a bathing cottage by the Blackburne family, of Hale hall. During the last war, Mrs.

Harry Johnson, wife of the keeper at that time, had the frightening experience of being machine-gunned by a German aircraft as she opened the lighthouse shutters. Bombs also landed near the lighthouse in another raid.

A fascinating piece of Old England is present at Hale in its 17th Century "duck decoy." This is a pentagon-shaped pond, built by wildfowlers in the middle of some salt marshes, which attracted thousands of ducks that flew in from places like Burton Marsh in Wirral. The decoy is now being restored by the Cheshire County Council for a completely opposite purpose — as a bird sanctuary.

One of the most fascinating customs at Hale — still strictly observed even today — is its office of Lord Mayor, stemming from a Charter granted by King John in 1203. The original office, apparently, was that of Constable, and the first man so appointed decided to create himself mayor in addition. So, Hale had a mayor for centuries and when Liverpool was upgraded to a city, little Hale, first with its charter, anyway, followed suit by also raising the mayoral status.

For many years, this village office — the only one in the country — goes to the longest-standing farmer on the squire's estate for the duration of his life. The robes and tricorn hat, which go with the job, are every bit as flamboyant as those of city Lord Mayors, not to mention the entourage of sword-bearer, mace-bearer, keeper-of-the-purse, keeper-of-records and a town crier!

Another fabulous custom of Hale's is creating its own Freemen, who get a plaque of the local coat of arms and a tie as tokens of this honour. A Freeman first must swear an ancient oath before the Lord Mayor — to the effect that he promises to be a thorough drinker, fair smoker and a dear lover of the fair sex!

WAVERTREE & EDGE HILL

THE discovery of burial urns, flint arrowheads and scrapers, suggesting a Stone Age settlement, makes *Wavertree* one of Liverpool's most historic districts, possibly linked with Calderstones. At the time of the Conquest it was known by names like Wartre (the syllable "tre" could be south Celtic for village, say some etymologists), Waudtre, Wavtre and even Wastpull and Wastyete. Domesday registers it as Wavretreu.

Other word experts seem quite certain that some forms of the name mean the gate or road over the waste as, indeed, the district was once part of the wild Childwall Heath, with heather, gorse, woods, sandstone outcrops and marshy depressions. Wastpull suggests a pool on the waste, and a small lake existed on the site of the present Village Green right up to 1928, when it was filled in and made into a children's playground. On the other hand, if we accept the Anglo-Saxon "waeffer" as roughly meaning vibrating, we could make out the name to represent "waving tree" — an aspen, perhaps?

Remains of what was probably part of a pre-Celtic settlement were found on Olive Mount (North Drive region) between Sandown Hall and Victoria Park, in July, 1867, by workmen laying foundations for a house. Six earthenware jars contained ashes and burnt bones and a few flint arrowheads and scrapers. Two more urns were found later. Large stones were nearby, some upright in the ground and the site was undoubtedly a megalithic tomb.

A local, unnamed historian, who declared that the Romans once occupied or passed through Wavertree, declared in 1910 that: "Wavertree people have gazed upon huge blocks of sandstone, marked by chariot wheels, in a great thoroughfare which runs across Victoria Park to Sandown." (See also Aigburth). He also refers to "Wavertree Lodge" as being one of King John's hunting lodges. He could be taking this building to be the lodge in Lodge Lane, but does not pinpoint the site. Describing the lodge, he states: "Its solid sandstone foundations and the fact that many of the intervening walls are composed of half trunks of trees, built with a curious plaster made in a bygone age, together with scraps of the house's subsequent history, all point to the truth of Wavertree's inclusion in John's great hunting forest."

Today, those living in the hub of Wavertree — round the Green and the Clock Tower — still regard this as "the village" and are justly proud of their district. The Green was once the venue for fairs, bull-baiting, cock-fighting and picnics, and it spread as far as Wavertree Nook. The little Round House on the Green (opposite the supermarket, which was once the Abbey Cinema), was an overnight lock-up, kept quite busy with drunks from the nearby hostelries and summertime fair revels. It was also used in 1832 as a temporary mortuary for cholera victims.

The house at the corner of the High Street and Waterloo Street, was once also used as a jail before a new police station was built nearly opposite on the High Street in 1873. A barred window may still be seen in the older building.

A few yards beyond the Round House and recreation ground lies the 570 years' old Monks' Well, with its Latin inscription translated as "He who does not give what he has, the Devil smiles below." Tunnels were said to have run from this site towards Childwall and Sandown. Some credence for the latter, perhaps, in that Long Lane collapsed in places as though undermined!

The railed-off Round House, as it looked in December, 1922.

The Monks' Well at Wavertree, reputed to be some 570 years' old.

The Picton Clock Tower, known locally as "Sarah Pooley," is a memorial to the lady of that name, who was the wife of Sir James Allanson Picton, Liverpool's greatest historian, an architect and well-known local dignitary. Built in 1884, it carries the inscription: "Time wasted is existence; used it is life." Picton Road and Picton Library also preserve this historian's name. The latter was the first public building in Liverpool to have electric lighting installed — introduced by Picton.

At No. 95 High Street stood the reputed smallest house in England — six feet wide and 14 feet deep, with two rooms. Families were raised in this cramped abode, incorporated in the Cock and Bottle public house in 1952.

The poetess Dorothea Hemans (chiefly remembered for Casabianca — "The boy stood on the burning deck...") lived at 17 High Street from 1828 to 1831. She was born Felicia Dorothea Brown, the daughter of George Brown, an Irish merchant and an Italian-German mother, at 32 (later 118) Duke Street, Liverpool, on September 25, 1793. When her father's business was failing, the family removed to Wales, where Felicia started writing poetry at the age of eight. Her first book of poems was published when she was only 15, and she later returned to Liverpool to live in Wavertree. She died in Dublin on May 16, 1836.

Between the wars, Olive Mount Children's Hospital, on the hill, was a complex of cottage homes accommodating 486 deprived children. Sixteen villas were each in the charge of a foster mother — like the Fazakerley Cottage Homes.

The smallest house in England, as it looked in 1933, jammed in between two buildings in Wavertree High Street. It is now part of the pub on the left.

An iron fence may now be seen between the pillars of the "gateway" in the wall bordering the site of former Wavertree Hall, in Church Road. The original, picturesque wrought-iron gates, which used to attract many artists, once opened on to the hall's driveway. The owners, says a local legend, in about the middle of the last century, locked this gate permanently and had the drive turfed over after their daughter eloped without their consent. This early 18th Century hall stood on the Cow Lane (now Prince Alfred Road) side of the grounds. When demolished in 1896, to make way for the present School for the Blind, the foundations of an even older building were discovered. Wavertree Hall was occupied in 1736 by Richard Percival, whose great-grandfather is said to have been the first man to be killed in the Civil War.

Two old pubs in the village are the Lamb and the Coffee House. The Lamb, with its oak-panelled interior, was recorded as long ago as 1754. The Coffee House is about 160 years old. Before the expansion of the city, huntsmen would meet on the common in front of the Coffee House for their stirrup-cups. Those were the days when the Jordan Brook crossed over Wavertree Road at Brook House Farm.

Development of Wavertree was slow and even by 1731 there were only 50 houses there. But its famous old church, Holy Trinity, drew its congregation from a wide radius. This church, now 190 years old, is thought to stand on the site of the ancient Chappell of Waretree. On one of its windows is, or was, scratched the date of the Battle of Waterloo. Someone must have prayed there in thanksgiving at the time. Stone mounting steps were available at each of the church's gates to give easier access to family coaches and horses. One set of steps still stands in Church Road near the church.

Well-worn mounting steps, opposite Holy Trinity Church.

Only a few yards from Holy Trinity is the bi-lateral Bluecoat School, opened at Wavertree in 1906. This was originally founded in School Lane, in the city, in 1708, as a charity school for 40 boys and 10 girls by the Rev. Robert Styth, the Rector of Liverpool. After a few years, it was decided to build a much larger school for 200 boys and 100 girls (generally poor or orphaned), to be lodged, fed and educated as inmates admitted at the age of nine and apprenticed at 14.

The new school was begun near the site of the original in 1716 and completed in 1726 at a cost of £2,000. This then was called the Blue Coat Hospital and was administered by about a hundred trustees. It still survives as the finest of Liverpool's ancient buildings and a monument to its kindly founder, Bryan Blundell, who was twice Mayor of Liverpool (1721 and 1728). The children were removed from School Lane to Wavertree in 1906.

Girl and boy pupils of the Bluecoat School at Wavertree wore the original uniforms right up to July, 1949, when the school's co-educational system ended after 241 years. Only boys have attended since. The girls used to wear blue frocks, with white linen tippets and cloaks for outdoors. The boys wore old-fashioned cut-away coats with silver buttons, heavy waistcoats and lawyer-like white tabs. In the city school, even in the late Victoria era, pupils were made to rise at 6 a.m. every day and scrub the white board floors spotless with sand and stone.

The Crown Mill at Wavertree (Mill Lane, one of the oldest routes, led to this) was the property of the monarchs reigning between 1475 and 1629. Then, King Charles I sold his rights in this, and the manor, to James, Lord Strange, son of the Earl of Derby. Other well-known local families, like the Ashburnhams, Greenes and Gascoynes, successively owned it. The son of the coachman who worked for Colonel Bourne, a local dignitary who once leased the mill, was killed when struck by the sails. Another child, the daughter of one of the millers, was scalped when her hair was caught up in the flailing sails. She was unconcious for 12 hours but recovered.

When local folk began to believe that an evil spirit, living in the quarry adjacent to this mill, had cursed the mill because of the accidents, its sails were set in a position to throw the shadow of a cross across the quarry when the sun was behind them. The quarry was filled in in 1877 and streets and houses now cover the site. Corn was ground at the Wavertree mill until 1889 and, in response to pleas in 1896 to preserve the old mill, the Marquess of Salisbury had the fabric repaired. However, its eventual end was near and in 1916 it was demolished. Its brick and sandstone foundations may still be seen at the top of Beverley Road, off Church Road.

The derelict Crown Mill, demolished in 1916.

Wavertree also embraces Liverpool's famous "Mystery" — the huge recreation and showground, originally donated to the city in May, 1895, as a children's playground by an anonymous citizen (hence the "mystery") but thought to have been Mr. Philip Holt.

Another extensive open space in the district is Botanic Park, on which stood a second Wavertree Hall, the residence of John Plumbe. A wealthy merchant and landowner, Plumbe built the hall in 1719 and his family lived there until 1823. It was eventually occupied by other residents, two of whom became Mayors of Liverpool. These were Mr. Charles Lawrence, Mayor in 1823-24, the first chairman of the Liverpool-Manchester Railway (after whom Lawrence Road was named), and Sir Joshua Walmsley, Mayor in 1839-40. When the Corporation bought the estate in 1843, with the intention of building a jail there, the hall was demolished. However, this idea was shelved and the land was neglected for 13 years, when it was decided to lay it out as a park. Liverpool Botanic Gardens were formed on part of this park in 1836. (See Calderstones).

Sandown Hall was once occupied by Hugh Hornby (Mayor of Liverpool in 1838) and wealthy trader who gave the land on which the original St. Mary's Church in Sandown Road was built in 1852. His name is remembered in Hornby Dock and the Hornby Library.

Brick and sandstone-built Edge Lane Hall, the frontage of which faced the Dogs' Home, off Edge Lane, was a 17th Century mansion with 17 bedrooms and large cellars. Little is known of its early history but it was occupied in 1835 by John Shaw Leigh, after whom Leigh Street, Liverpool, is said to have been named.

Prince Arthur, Queen Victoria's last surviving son and the first Duke of Connaught and Strathearn, once spent a week-end in Wavertree as the guest of Mr. S. R. Graves, M.P., at his home, The Grange. The Prince was in Liverpool officially to open Sefton Park. He was met at Broadgreen Station on Saturday, May 18, 1872 and, escorted by a detachment of Dragoon Guards, entered the village through a triumphal arch to be presented with an address by J. A. Picton, the historian already mentioned, who was also chairman of the local Board. Later Sir James Picton, he lived at Sandy Knowe on Mill Lane, Olive Mount, now converted into flats.

Crowds lined the six-mile route taken by the Prince on the Monday, when he made a tour of the city before driving to the park for the opening ceremony in a procession of 77 carriages. Prince Arthur had visited this park some time earlier, after its purchase, to review volunteer troops there. It was intended to stage a large-scale mock battle with artillery and cavalry charges for his benefit. But, (laughably for many), hundreds of spectators invaded the "battleground" and brought the charge to a ridiculous walk. People even sat astride the cannon! The Prince was amused, too.

Wavertree had its rural ghosts, and in the last century many of the villagers who lived in their delightful old cottages would recall the stories of the ghost of a local farmer, sitting in his porch on a midsummer evening, smoking his long churchwarden pipe . . . and the more terrifying tales of the midnight drives of the dreaded 'Childwall Coach," with its panting steeds!

Red Indians once came to Wavertree and actually did their shopping in Wavertree Road. That was in about 1906, when they were here as part of Buffalo Bill's (Colonel William Cody) rodeo from America, then making another tour of Europe. (See also Newsham district for Cody's first visit).

This show played to packed houses in the huge Tournament Hall on the Exhibition Ground between Edge Lane and Wavertree Road, on the site now occupied by the Corporation's Edge Lane bus depot. Its main entrance was opposite Garthowen Road.

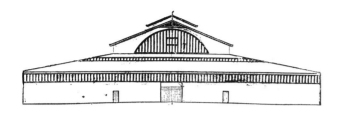

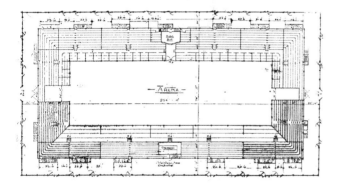

Above: The frontage of Tournament Hall, which occupied two acres. Below: The hall's huge arena, where many spectacular shows and exhibitions were staged. This also incorporated a royal box and an area for a large orchestra. Performers could make their entries from a number of aisles leading from an avenue running around the interior of the hall at the back of the blocks of tiered seats.

The last time that North American Indians came to Liverpool was on October 25, 1926, when five of the Sioux tribe arrived in the city to promote the film "The Flaring Frontier." Dressed in their full regalia, they included Chief Eagle Elk (grandson of Sitting Bull), his squaw and three thousand braves. The chief was unable to ride the horse provided for him because he had broken his arm when thrown from his horse the week before at Nottingham. A car was placed at his disposal. Eagle Elk had visited Liverpool in the spring that year, when he backed Jack Horner in the Grand National. He was a good judge of horses, for Jack Horner won!

Tournament Hall was a massive white building which could accommodate some 15,000 people. Built by Isaac Dixon, of the Windsor Iron Works, Edge Hill, with a frame of cast-iron and walls of corrugated iron, its glass roof and glass lantern lighting gave it the "Crystal Palace touch."

This hall was the venue of many major Liverpool shows and exhibitions, including probably the city's first-ever motor show in 1907. But the first "purpose-built" exhibition hall to be constructed in that area was made from the iron framework of an Antwerp exhibition building. This accommodated Liverpool's International Exhibition of Navigation, Commerce and Manufacture, opened by Queen Victoria on May 11, 1886.

The Exhibition Hall, as this was called, was the main feature of a number of buildings covering a 10-acre site. It had a 100ft. high dome and overlooked Wavertree Park and the Botanic Gardens. Access to it was via newly-laid "Exhibition Road," with entrances from Wavertree Road and Edge Lane. A platform was specially built on the adjacent railway line for the Queen's arrival by overnight train from Windsor.

One of Liverpool's most historic occasions – the opening of the Liverpool and Manchester Railway, on September 15, 1830, sketched by a contemporary artist. Picture shows the Moorish Arch at Edge Hill and the Prime Minister, the Duke of Wellington's coach on the left.

Wavertree and particularly *Edge Hill* have considerable important links with the world-renowned Liverpool — Manchester Railway, built by George Stephenson, which began the "Railway Age" right here in Liverpool with its opening on September 15, 1830. This was the first public railway to be steam-hauled throughout and it set the standards for future main-line development.

In the early days of this railway, a burly Scot used to man the level-crossing at Wavertree Lane (Leigh Road, near the junction of Wavertree Road and Botanic Road, led to this).

He lived in a cottage, now the site of the gasworks in Spofforth Road, and kept an eye on this section of the track, hurrying tardy folk across the rails with a long whip!

Lime Street Station opened on August 15, 1836, six years after the railway started. But the first Liverpool passenger terminus was at Crown Street. During that interim period, passengers were conveyed between Crown Street and the town, via Myrtle Street (then open ground), by horse-drawn buses and coaches to join their train carriages.

Edge Hill Station was the locomotive terminus at Liverpool and the carriages were hauled by endless rope (driven by a stationary steam-engine at Edge Hill) into the higher level Crown Street Station. Travelling in the opposite direction, trains were dispatched, with passengers, from

Edge Hill Station. Its sandstone buildings formed part of the original station.

Crown Street by gravity through a single-bore tunnel down to Edge Hill, where they were attached to the locomotives, waiting in what has been described as the "Grand Area," resplendent with a fine Moorish Arch. This is now known as the Chatsworth Street cutting.

Even for some years after Lime Street Station was opened and the passenger traffic transferred there from Crown Street, carriages still had to be rope-drawn through a tunnel to Edge Hill and the waiting engines. This system operated until the 1890's, when the locomotives became sufficiently powerful to haul the trains under their own steam.

A poster announcing the opening of the new railway in 1830, stipulated, among other now-fascinating data on the timetable, rules and regulations, etc., that the staff, including porters, were forbidden to accept tips under threat of instant dismissal!

The 1829 "Stephenson" tunnel-mouth now lies buried beneath rubble since the landscaping of the old Crown Street Station site. Apparently this was done to stabilise Smithdown Lane, elevated at this point. In April, 1955, workmen digging in the then Crown Street goods-yard, uncovered some rails which many of Stephenson's locomotives must have run upon. These 125-year-old rails were supported by heavy stone slabs.

Probably Edge Hill's best-known resident was Joseph Williamson, dubbed the "King" and the "Mole" of this district, under which he made a bewildering labyrinth of useless rooms and tunnels through the underlying sandstone. Although he might be described as a modern troglodite and an eccentric, Williamson, a wealthy tobacco merchant, spent an estimated £100,000 in paying unemployed men from this district to dig these tunnels — some of which opened out into huge caverns with brick-lined vaulted roofs. No one has ever determined why he did this, other than from sincere altruism, but he certainly left behind him a headache for our city planners . . . his weird excavations still continue to be rediscovered. He even lived in a cellar himself, for the sitting-room in his house in Mason Street was nothing more than a long vault with a window at one end, and his bedroom, at the back of this, was simply an adjoining cave.

When once asked what his motive was, he replied: "Employment of the poor, for if you give them something to do, no matter what, it keeps them out of mischief."

Joseph was born at Warrington on March 10, 1769. He obtained work with a tobacco merchant, named Thomas Moss Tate, in Wolstenholme Square, and later married Betty Tate, his employer's daughter. He was almost two persons. Generally, he wore an old patched coat, corduroy breeches and heavy, sloppy shoes. He could be uncouth, rough and gruff. Yet, socially, he would draw himself up to his full muscular six feet, dress in the finest clothes like any gentlemen of his day, his handsome face would smile and he presented himself as a very distinguished person. When a Royal Duke once visited Liverpool Williamson bowed as he passed. The Duke was impressed and inquired who it was who had made "the most courtly bow I have seen out of St. James'!"

Williamson read the Bible, was very fond of children and a great friend of the poor. It was said that he never sold any of the stone he had excavated and that St. Jude's Church was built from some of this. He also built other houses in the district, including some in High Street, Edge Hill. One of those houses had a cellar which could have accommodated 200 tons of coal!

His tunnelling impressed even railway engineer Stephenson, who was in Liverpool at that time. Stephenson inspected some of Williamson's excavations and declared that these, in their way, were some of the most astonishing works he had ever seen. But Williamson allowed very few strangers to see his works. "These are not show shops and I am not a showman," he would growl.

When Stephenson's men were cutting the tunnel from Edge Hill to Lime Street, in about 1834, the ground suddenly gave way beneath them. And there, below, was Williamson and some of his "moles" digging their own tunnel below the official one. Williamson told the amazed navvies (who must have thought they had discovered Hades) that "if they wanted to know how to tunnel, he could give them a lesson in that polite art."

For some time Wapping Tunnel was gas-lit and people were allowed to walk through it from Edge Hill to Wapping Station at the dockside.

Joe once built what must have been the strangest house in Liverpool, on the corner of Bolton Street. This was square, with basement, ground floor, first floor and with huge windows. It was also minus a kitchen. A tunnel ran from its cellar under Mason Street to vaults opposite. He built this as a studio for an artist friend who had complained about the poor light he had to work in. Joe couldn't understand when the artist tried to explain that it was the quality of light not the quantity of it that he needed. The house was never occupied.

In all his weird designs and buildings, Williamson never had any plans or drawings and his men would simply work on until told to stop.

Many amusing stories must have been recounted about Joe Williamson, but the one which seems to have lasted down the years is about the time that he invited a party of gentlefolk to dine with him. He showed his guests into one of his bare rock rooms, in which he had placed a trestle table and forms for seats. Each guest was faced with a plate of porridge and some hard ships' biscuits — and all were invited to tuck in! Some, feeling highly insulted, left the room and Williamson bowed them out. Then, smiling at those who had stayed, Joe opened up some dividing doors and ushered them into a delightful room with a veritable banquet prepared for them. There was a big laugh, followed by big eats.

Williamson, in fact, was very hospitable and would serve his visitors with mugs and jugs full of wine rather than in small glasses. He even provided beer for his tunnelling workers.

One section of his land, near Grinfield Street, was completely undermined in overlapping passages and galleries. A brick-lined excavation, which opened on to a garden in Smithdown Lane (the western boundary of

Williamson's land) was some 15ft. high and broad enough to take two carts side by side. It went deep into the rock and opened up as a cavern 26ft. high. Another vault was 36ft. wide and 30ft. high, and yet another arch, 60ft high. Houses in Mason Street used to rest on such brick arches, the depth of the excavations for which could be seen through grids.

Part of Williamson's labyrinth, piled with rubble.

Joe Williamson died on May 1, 1840, aged 71, from "water on the chest." He was buried with his wife (who died 18 years earlier) in the graveyard of old St. Thomas's Church, which stood on a triangular piece of land at the junction of Paradise Street and Park Lane. This was the same church in which they were married, when Joe turned up for the wedding in his hunting pink and, after the ceremony, sent his wife home to prepare a meal while he went off to join the Liverpool Hunt!

With such a start to their married life, small wonder that they constantly quarrelled. It is said that, after one row, Joe released all the birds from his wife's aviary, shouting how many a man would relish such freedom!

St. Thomas's Church was once very popular, attended by many wealthy Liverpool families in the early days, before the district around it became a mass of dockside back streets, with numerous inns, taverns, and ale-houses, some no bigger than a cottage, and where, between Parliament Street and Great George's Street, some 28,000 people were living in squalor by 1828. When built in 1750, it was only the fourth church in Liverpool and boasted a 216ft. spire.

For nearly 30 years, from 1870, a woman known as "Silent Jane" regularly attended this church. Her real name was Jane Redfern and although obviously well-educated, her life and background remained a complete mystery. She never spoke to a soul, yet in church she would join in the hymns and chants, singing beautifully. Alone in her room, she would sometimes sing or speak to herself in a rich, refined voice.

After the church was demolished in 1906 and all the other human remains had been exhumed and removed, the vault containing the Williamsons was left undisturbed. For many years this was surrounded by a privet hedge. And there they still lie, beneath what is now a car-park . . . a very poor monument to such an incredible Liverpool character, who aided so many of the town's destitute during his lifetime.

The property belonging to this "Mole of Edge Hill" was chiefly held under the Waste Lands Commission and his leases expired in 1858, when some of the most elaborate parts of his labyrinth were closed and sealed off. There are still plans of part of this Edge Hill maze, but the exact locations of all the excavations (many were filled in) are unknown. During the last war it was considered using some of these as air-raid shelters, but the plan did not materialise.

Mason Street, where Williamson lived and from where most of the tunnelling began, was named after another resident there, Edward Mason. He was a timber merchant and his house, built at the end of the 18th Century, had a huge garden stretching all the way down to Smithdown Lane. Mason paid for the building of St. Mary's Church, Edge Hill.

A 1768 map shows Edge Hill ending at the west side of present Hall Lane. This area, including the site of St. Mary's and the "village green," then displayed a large band of deep outcrop sandstone, called "Cheetham's Brow," which later became Hall Lane. The area probably derived its name from being simply the hill at the start of Edge Lane, the old highway known as such for countless years and the boundary dividing West Derby and Wavertree.

From the "edge" of Edge Hill, in the early part of the last century and before, one could look down on ancient Moss Lake Fields, which lay between Myrtle Street and Paddington and from the top of Mount Pleasant to the rise of Edge Hill. The Moss Lake Brook, or "gutter" as this was called, ran through these fields, where Grove Street now is, spreading out as a large pond on the site of the junction with Oxford Street. This stretch of water was also a favourite resort of skaters during hard frosts.

Where the Royal William public house now stands (the same or an earlier pub there was once called the King William Tavern), at the junction of Crown Street with Pembroke Place, was a stile. This led to the Moss Lake area, once used as a "turbary," or turf-field, where people collected peat for their fires. Part of the turbary, drained in 1809, became Abercromby Square.

Many fine houses were built in Edge Hill in the 1830's, around the "Green," known as Holland Place. And from this centre, on May 2, 1885, a little bit of cycling history was made. Thomas Stevens, an Anglo-American long-distance cyclist, who had arrived in Liverpool from San Francisco via Boston, set out on the second lap of his journey round the world — on his bone-shaking penny-farthing bicycle — watched by several hundred people. He was the first round-the-world cyclist.

Part of Liverpool's "inner-circle" route, between Wavertree Road and Kensington — Durning Road and Holt Road — are named after landowner William Durning and his son-in-law, George Holt, whose name is also associated with the Liverpool Institute and Blackburne House.

WEST DERBY & CROXTETH

AS one of the eight Hundreds of Lancashire, West Derby was far more important than the little hamlet of Liverpool, ignored by the Domesday survey. Fifteen townships were under its jurisdiction and its old boundaries came as far west into the Liverpool area as Moss Street, Islington. The word "Boundary" associated with Liverpool street names generally refers to West Derby's influential spread. Its early name, Derbei or Deorby, comes from the Old Norse "dyr" and Anglo-Saxon "deor," meaning deer, to which the Scandinavian suffix "by" is added. Like Derby in the Midlands, which has the same roots, it was a good hunting place.

At the time of the Danish settlers and through Anglo-Saxon times until the 13th Century, it stood in a huge forest, some 11 miles long and two miles wide, stretching from Thornton to Blackbrook, St. Helens. West Derby still remained very wooded even after 1224, when many of the forests were cleared for agriculture.

A Saxon fort stood there for some 200 years, followed by a small Norman motte-and-bailey fort, said to have been built by Count Roger de Poitu. King Richard I held this castle in 1197, and Edmund, Earl of Lancaster, in 1296. It once had a garrison of ten knights and crossbowmen and 140 foot soldiers. But the castle was allowed to decay when Liverpool's more robust fortress was built and, in about 1826, old timbers and hewn stones were excavated from its site on the now-landscaped Castle Green. An oak beam dug from this ruin was made into a writing-desk for Mr. J. McGeorge, of Everton, at that time.

This walled, circular garden marks the site of West Derby's ancient castle.

King John transferred the Wapentake Court from West Derby in 1207, when he granted his Charter to Liverpool. These courts dealt with business-like land tenures, freeholds and leases, and became the county courts of today. Wapentake means "weapon-touch." When the Sergeant of the Hundred held his court, he would stick his spear into the ground and the liege men would touch this with their swords as a sign of fealty.

After King Charles I sold West Derby, it passed into the hands of Lord Strange (the Earl of Derby executed at Bolton) and eventually to the Marquess of Salisbury.

A serious incident in West Derby in July, 1424, is seen as amusing in retrospect. Sir Richard Molyneux and Sir Thomas Stanley were preparing to fight each other with their respective armies, numbering about 2,000 each, when the

Sheriff, acting on a writ from King Henry IV arrested both knights, sending Stanley to Kenilworth and Molyneux to Windsor. Their quarrel, however, was soon made up. They and their successors, through to the late last Earl of Sefton and the present Earl of Derby, continued to be good friends.

There are still many old buildings in West Derby Village (now a conservation area), like the Manor Court House, dated 1662, and the slightly older Yeoman's Cottage, of 1600.

The old Wapentake Court, West Derby, now conserved.

Bull-baiting and cock-fighting drew big crowds on market days and at the times of the "Wakes," the local inns thrived. In the mid-16th Century they were open 24 hours a day and strong beer was only ½d a pint!

Some Liverpool sailors, out on a spree in the village, freed a bull being baited by dogs. They took it into the Theatre Royal, Williamson Square, Liverpool, "to show him the play."

Liverpool's old Theatre Royal – patronised by a bull.

There was much wassailing in those days and the stocks often accommodated a drunk. The stocks in the old animal pound by the Yeoman's Cottage display an iron replica of the original. A local drunk, named "Peg-Leg Harry," is recorded as having been locked in the stocks in the 1830's and pelted with rotten fruit. This treatment, of course, was not always as funny as it might appear and sometimes unfortunate victims were badly injured.

Ecclesiastically, West Derby was part of Walton Parish for many years but became independent in 1848. Its present Parish Church, built in 1853-54, to the design of Mr. (later Sir) Gilbert G. Scott, took the place of the ancient Chapel of St. Mary the Virgin, which stood in the village centre. Heywood's Monument now marks its altar site.

By the Parish Church runs a path which leads to *Croxteth Hall*, former seat of the Earls of Sefton, the Molyneux family. This family was one of the oldest in the kingdom, associated with Liverpool since 1296 and governors of the Liverpool Castle for centuries. It descended from William de Molines who, at the time of the Conquest, obtained a grant of Sefton. In July, 1446, Henry VI granted to Richard Molyneux of Sefton, the parks of Croxteth and Toxteth and the forest of Simonswood.

Croxteth Hall became the Molyneuxes' residence from the reign of Edward IV. This is a magnificent, chiefly 18th Century mansion, embodying other periods, including the oldest, Elizabethan. A stone in the wall of an out-building is inscribed "C.M. 1687." The initials are those of Caryll, third Viscount Molyneux who, 43 years earlier, commanded the Royalist troops who were the first to breach Liverpool's defences when Prince Rupert captured the town in the Civil War.

British and foreign royalty have visited and stayed at Croxteth Hall during its occupation by the Earls. One, in 1812, was "Compte d'Artois," the exile name of the King of France, who became Charles X when Napoleon was sent to

Croxteth Hall, nestled among its ancestral trees before its great estate became public parkland.

Elba. The King, the Duc de Berri (Commander-in-Chief, French Army) and many other royal personages of the French and English Courts, used to pray at the R.C. Chapel of St. Swithin in nearby *Gill Moss*. This was a converted loft beneath a group of 18th Century cottages, where Mass was said regularly for 56 years. The chapel, close to the old Church of St. Swithin (rebuilt 1969), was dedicated by the late Dr. Richard Downey (Archbishop of Liverpool), in May, 1952, as a shrine to the Lancashire martyrs.

Croxteth Hall was presented to the Merseyside County Council in 1974 by the late Lady Sefton. Opened to the public in September, 1976, it is now a popular and attractive museum, within a large country park, containing gardens, lake and animals.

One of Merseyside's oldest thoroughfares is that running between Sefton Village and Croxteth Hall, which used to pass through Netherton, once a hamlet of Sefton.

West Derby has four mills, including a horse-mill and a water-mill in the castle area. Millbank and the Jolly Miller public house conserves the name of a windmill on that spot at the top of the hill. And Acker's Mill was on the Prescot Road side of the village. (See Dovecot).

The yew tree, which gave its name to the cemetery and the lane in West Derby, grew in a local garden. This could have been 1,000 years old or more. The owners had a timber bower built among its mighty branches and they would sit there and drink tea on warm summer days.

Bellefield, Everton F.C.'s training ground, by Sandfield Park, was originally the home of Sir Edward Bates, founder of the famous Liverpool shipping family long associated with the Cunard Line. This great Gothic-style house, with leaded lights and long driveway to the entrance, over which was displayed a coat of arms, stood empty and derelict for about 30 years until the Cunard Company took over the ground as a sports field.

Tysons, the builders, bought this land in 1934 for £9,500, and Mr. Leslie Tyson, when he was 75, told me that because cash was demanded in payment, he had to draw from the bank nine £1,000 notes and a £500 note. He carried these in his pocket and went by taxi to the negotiating solicitor, protected by "the biggest joiner we employed!" Everton rented the ground after the war and finally bought the freehold in 1960.

Melwood, Liverpool F.C.'s training ground nearby, was originally a farm field. The Jesuit Order took it over in about 1920 and it served as the sports ground for St. Francis Xavier's College until 1951 when, according to former Liverpool F.C. manager, Mr. Bob Paisley, his club bought it.

While on the subject of sport in this district, for a long time after the war the Americans from Burtonwood would play baseball with local teams in Beavans Lane.

Have you ever noticed how everyone in West Derby seems to live in roads, avenues, lanes and drives? What happened to streets?

Sandfield Park, with its rare trees, was once a private residential area virtually surrounded by countryside until new buildings encroached on its sylvan setting. A toll of a penny a wheel was levied on vehicles driven through it, and, as a private area, it had to close to traffic for 24 hours once a year. Collections now are either very infrequent or have lapsed. This park took its name from an ancient house, now called The Old Hall, parts of which are said to date from 1635.

WOOLTON & GATEACRE

CAMP Hill, *Woolton*, one of the city's southern beauty spots, has long been a popular place for local walks and picnics. But probably few know that this 250ft. hill, part of a sandstone ridge (its neighbouring hill is 295 ft.) once supported an Iron Age camp or fort — possibly occupied by some of the Brigantes. The Anglo-Saxons (and perhaps the Vikings, too) obviously appreciated its geographical features, with aesthetically and militarily-appealing views of the river, the peninsular and the Welsh Mountains. It seems likely that one of them, maybe a Teutonic chief named Wulf or Ulf, who settled in this wooded, rocky and marshy area and cultivated some of it, created its name.

As Wulf's or Ulf's "tun" (farmstead) is Anglo-Saxon, Domesday records the districts of Little Woolton (Gateacre) and Much Woolton (Woolton Village), respectively, as Ulvetune and Uvetone. Some folk have presumed that these names derived from the animal wolf and that the area must have been the haunt of wolves. But the former explanation is probably correct.

Gateacre probably means the "road to the field," from the Middle English gate, meaning "way", or the Scandinavian "gata" and the Anglo-Saxon "acre" (field). Gateacre Brow, a former track and one of the village's ancient central crossroads, could have been the "way" to the grazing land on the high common although some interpret the name as "goat field," and even as "God's acre," from the Anglo-Saxon "Gottesacker."

When thanes and knights held so much of the land, the Woolton farmsteads were valued at an annual sum of 158 pence (denarii). Little Woolton, with its two carucates of land and half a league of woods, was worth 62 pence; Much Woolton, with one carucate of land, 30 pence, and Wilaldeslie (or Wibald's Lee) — thought to be present Lee Park — 64 pence.

A "carucate" is a large piece of land, rather difficult to assess in area, but said to be "as much as could be tilled with one plough and eight oxen in a year. The state of the ground, therefore, must have made a big difference to the sizes of a carucate!

Woolton has passed through many ownerships, including the Knights of St. John of Jerusalem (who held the manor for about 300 years, until Henry VIII dissolved the order in 1540); Queen Elizabeth; Robert of Upholland; James I; the 6th Earl of Derby; Isaac Green, the Liverpool lawyer, and the Marquess of Salisbury. Today, Woolton and Gateacre, both of which came within the Liverpool boundary in 1913, support large and thriving communities.

A number of those living thereabouts, particularly the Woolton Society, whose abundant literature on the area has been a most helpful adjunct to my own notes, are striving hard to preserve the heritage of these villages, many of whose old properties happily are being conserved. In 1969, Liverpool City Council declared the centre of Gateacre a conservation area.

Woolton once boasted a watermill. Built by the Hospitallers early in the 14th Century, this is thought to have stood on Childwall Brook, just below Naylor's Bridge at the

49

end of Childwall Valley Road. The stream obviously had more pressure then than it has had for most of this century! A windmill, in Church Road, built about 1811 and converted to steam-drive in 1835, was burnt down in a gale on March 24, 1898.

The sandstone quarry in Woolton has given a good deal of employment in its time. Much of its stone has gone into the building of Liverpool's Anglican Cathedral, as well as other important buildings and, of course, local structures.

The population of Woolton almost doubled last century, when newcomers from many parts of Britain and Ireland settled there. Many Irish folk moved in following the mass migrations at the time of the potato famine. During the severe cold of December, 1874, when so many people were workless, the local religious leaders arranged for a soup kitchen to feed some 450 villagers twice daily for eleven days. Total cost: £40!

In addition to its agricultural achievements, Woolton was also famous for its pig-breeding and some good specimens were regularly marketed on the site of the High Street.

A number of 18th Century buildings and cottages remain in Woolton village to help maintain its Old Worlde atmosphere. Its tiny and ancient school is now a showpiece. Although dated 1610, it could be even older and is said to be one of the earliest elementary schools in Britain. One historian reckoned that this school was founded between 1630 and the outbreak of the Civil War, but does not say who endowed or founded it. Another historical account refers to "a grammar school now abandoned, was founded in the 16th Century"; there is a record of Robert Quick, "schoolmaster,"

The old school at Woolton, as it appeared in about 1930.

who wrote up the Childwall Registers in 1597-98; and Edward Norris, of Speke, who died in 1606, left £60 in his will to provide a schoolmaster at Woolton. At least, it has been established that this school was operating in 1625.

Father John Almond, born in Allerton about 1567, who, although taken to Dublin in 1575 to avoid persecution, was eventually martyred at Tyburn and canonised in 1970, said at his trial that he went to school in Woolton. Could this little school have been the one? Some authorities believe that originally it was a pre-Reformation chapel. It has also served as a cottage, cowshed and barn.

Another gem is 18th Century Woolton Hall, in Speke Road, now a Grade 1 listed building. This was built in 1704 for Viscount Molyneux and enlarged in 1772 by Nicholas Ashton, a Liverpool shipping and salt merchant and former

Woolton Hall.

High Sheriff of Lancashire. It is said to contain Lancashire's only example of Robert Adam's work. He remodelled the interior and designed the carriage front. Among distinguished visitors who dined at Woolton Hall were Lord Cardington (1718) and Nicholas Blundell, Crosby's famous diarist-squire. Although Woolton Hall is said to have been built in the year stated, there might well have been a much older building, or part of it, incorporated within its structure at that time. The mystery is posed by the report of author and poet Samuel Derrick (appointed Master of the Ceremonies at Bath after the death of Beau Nash in 1761, and also M.C. at Tunbridge Wells), who visited Liverpool in 1760 to write about some of the villages and stately homes there.

"The most remarkable of these," he wrote, "is the dwellinghouse of Lord Molyneux, which is small and neat, constructed of rude iron-coloured stone, and in appearance about two hundred years old . . ." That observation could put a date of 1560 on Woolton Hall! Some old tunnels (priest bolt-holes?) running under parts of Woolton are said to start from the south-east corner of this hall.

Probably the oldest relic in the area is Woolton Cross (now repaired), thought to have been erected by the Knights Hospitaller.

Another mediaeval cross used to stand relatively near to this, in the adjoining (now vanished) hamlet of *Hunt's Cross*. According to the Victoria History of the County of Lancaster, the remains of Hunt's Cross were described in 1895 as "a displaced massive square stone socket, lying in a barn at the crossroads near the station." The remnants of this cross — "the stump of a shaft on a cube stone base sitting on two square stone steps," — may now be seen at the junction of Hillfoot Avenue and Hillfoot Road.

The village cross at Woolton is linked with the Knights Hospitallers.

Two of the oldest pubs, of 17th Century origin, are the Coach and Horses and the Coffee House.

The first St. Peter's Church, opened in 1826 to cope with the increasing population of the parish, was demolished to make way for the new St. Peter's, opened in 1887.

Before electric tramways linked Woolton with Liverpool (the village terminus was the stop for those alighting to visit popular Woolton Woods), a horse-drawn bus left the Coffee House for the city every hour. A driver of one of the latter, Ivan Davies, who wore a three-cornered hat, was nicknamed "Jehu" because of the fast and reckless manner in which he drove through the country lanes!

The cuckoo-clock, in the Old English Garden of Woolton Woods, was first started on June 29, 1927. An amplifier, hidden in the trees, produced the intriguing bird-call. Similar to one built in Edinburgh, this cuckoo-clock has contained as many as 14,000 plants at one time. It was made by a firm from that city and was presented to Liverpool by the family of the late Lt. Col. J. B. Gaskell who, as a boy, lived at the mansion on Woolton Woods estate.

Picturesque *Gateacre*, closely associated with Woolton, and now so built-up, was very much an isolated village among the

Gateacre Village still preserves much of its Old World charm.

farms at the turn of this century and later. Gateacre Village Institute, founded for the social recreation of youths and men from the village, was given to the township by Sir Andrew Barclay Walker. A Scot, who succeeded his father as owner of Peter Walker's Warrington Brewery, he came to Gateacre in 1865 and rebuilt The Grange as his residence. Another building had stood on this site about a century earlier.

Sir Andrew also gave Gateacre its Green, library and reading room, but his greatest gift is the magnificent Walker Art Gallery for the building of which he gave £20,000 during his Mayoralty in 1873. Walker was Mayor of Liverpool again in 1876-77, being knighted in the latter year, when the gallery was opened by Lord Derby and a public holiday was declared in Liverpool. He was also a High Sheriff of Lancashire and was made a baronet in 1886.

Sir Andrew Walker was the father of Lord Wavertree, Colonel William Hall Walker, who played a prominent part in the military, municipal, parliamentary and business life of Liverpool and was given a peerage in 1919. Lord Wavertree became the joint managing director of the family business and was a great sportsman, being an authority on horse-breeding and racing. He often entertained members of the racing fraternity when living at The Grange.

The stables which he originally built in 1895 for his string of polo ponies, were taken over in 1936 by Mr. Jim Blundell, as Gateacre Riding School, after they had lain empty for more than 20 years. Today, these have been converted into attractive cottages called "Grange Mews." The nearby houses in Paradise Row, date from about the 16th Century and are probably the oldest remaining houses in the village. Soarer Cottages in Grange Lane, dated 1896, were named after Lord Wavertree's horse, which won the Grand National that year.

Although a person who would help anyone down on his luck, Lord Wavertree did not believe in continuing to aid lame dogs indefinitely. He once declined to help a relative because his horoscope revealed that this was inadvisable! In 1915, he made a gift to the British Government of the national stud he kept in Ireland.

Lord Wavertree, who married Sheridan's great, great grand-daughter, died, aged 76, on February 2, 1933, leaving no heir to the title.

Chorley-born Sir Henry Tate, the prosperous Liverpool sugar-refiner, lived in Woolton for some years. He founded the huge Tate and Lyle refinery. A great philanthropist, he presented the nation with his collection of 65 fine paintings and £80,000 in cash to house them. This formed the nucleus of the Tate Gallery, founded in 1897. Perhaps Henry took his cue from Sir Andrew's gesture, 20 years earlier. Henry became a Freeman of Liverpool in 1891, was knighted seven years later and died in 1899, aged 80.

Another Wooltonian to be remembered was George Hunter Robertson, J.P., a member of the Little Woolton Local Board, who started the Lancashire Telephone Exchange Company. His office telephone number was Liverpool 1.

Abbot's Lea, in Beaconsfield Road, the large Victorian Gothic-style mansion, for many years a school for physically-handicapped children, stands on part of the land that once was Little Woolton Common. Among its tenants have been John Bushby, a Liverpool shipowner; William Gossage, the soap manufacturer, and Sir Benjamin Johnson, of the dye-works and cleaners' fame.

Widnes-born William Winwood Gossage, grandson of the founder of this famous soap firm, died here on August 28,

1934. He followed his father, Mr. F. H. Gossage into the family business in 1912, when living at Abbot's Lea. William was Mayor of Widnes in 1901-02 and fifth in a line of Widnes mayors of which his father was the first in 1892-93. His first wife was Miss Hannah Keen, daughter of Arthur Keen, the steel manufacturer. After her death, he married Miss Ethel Tate, daughter of Sir William Henry Tate, the sugar manufacturer.

Sir Ben Johnson, a former Mayor of Bootle and a Liberal, fought for the Kirkdale constituency, losing to Sir George Baden-Powell (the Chief Scout's elder brother), who was the M.P. from 1895 to 1898. Among the important offices Johnson held were Director of the Royal Army Clothing Department, High Sheriff of Lancaster and a Deputy Lieutenant of the County.

The fountain on the Green is an 1883 memorial to Councillor John Hays Wilson, a brass founder, who lived at Lee Hall till his death in 1881. He was chairman of the Liverpool Water Committee at the time the scheme for piping water from Lake Vyrnwy to Liverpool was planned.

Gateacre Hall, Halewood Road, thought to have been originally built about the middle of the 17th Century, has been altered considerably and is now a hotel. This has what is called The Slave Gate — a wrought-iron gate, taken from the site now occupied by Tower Building at the foot of Water Street. Slaves were reputed to have passed through this gate into the older Tower building there, where they were confined pending transhipment. Some slaves certainly were sold in Liverpool, but in spite of the sensational stories of waterfront cellars with ring-bolts, chains and so on, very few slaves actually passed through the port, being shipped from Africa directly to the Americas and West Indies.

The hall, once called The Nook, was a private boarding-school for some time in the middle of the last century. One of its owners, who did much to restore the property, was Mr. Edward C. R. Litler-Jones who, in June, 1937, was found shot dead in a hotel at Paarl, South Africa, where he had gone after a nervous breakdown. The managing director of Flett's jam factory, he had also been the youngest-ever member of Liverpool City Council.

Another delightful old building in Gateacre is the Unitarian Chapel, licensed in 1700 and once known as Little Lee Chapel. This "was recorded for a meeting place for an Assembly of Protestants dissenting from the Church of England for the Exercise of their religious worship . . .".

On what is now Lee Park Golf Club, stood Lee Hall, owned by the Okill family and built in 1773 by John Okill, shipbuilder and timber merchant. When owned by Councillor John Hays Wilson, its lovely gardens and parkland were opened to the public, and in the period 1881-83, the Tarbock Races were run in its grounds. These were organised by the Toxteth Hunt Club. Councillor Wilson's death was attributed to his catching cold at the races that year.

In 1869, the grounds of this hall were the venue of 100,000 people who visited the park to celebrate Orange Day. Dr. Richard Caton, Lord Mayor of Liverpool in 1907-08, and Pro-Chancellor of Liverpool University in 1922, was another tenant of Lee Hall, demolished in 1956.

Gateacre has a number of old pubs, too. The Black Bull and the Bear and Staff both probably date from the 18th Century, while the Brown Cow was converted from two early 19th Century cottages.